STRATEGIC SOVEREIGN WEALTH FUND (SWF) INVESTMENTS AS A POSSIBLE SOLUTION IN THE WAR OF RESOURCES

Is a strategic SWF investment an adequate instrument for national governments to secure access to critical raw material and energy inputs?

Marcel C. Tiemann

This publication is part of the master dissertation for the degree of M. Sc. at the
University of Leeds — Leeds University Business School

Supervised by Professor Peter Buckley, Professor of International Business,
Head of the International Business Division and Director of the
Centre for International Business at the University of Leeds (CIBUL).

Bibliografische Information der Deutschen Nationalbibliothek

Die Deutsche Nationalbibliothek verzeichnet diese Publikation in der
Deutschen Nationalbibliografie; detaillierte bibliografische Daten sind im Internet
über http://dnb.d-nb.de abrufbar.

1. Aufl. - Göttingen : Cuvillier, 2012

978-3-95404-082-7

Abstract

This publication examines Europe's strong dependency on importing essential minerals and metals for their industries and if a strategic European Union Sovereign Wealth Fund (EUSWF) is a possible solution for investing directly in producing countries in order to maximize the security of supply. This would be advanced measures for the "Raw Materials Initiative" (RMI) which has been launched by the European Commission in 2008 to react to the future development of minerals and metals which faced a scarcity based on natural limitation and increasing prices. Both are driven by a global shift from western economies to eastern economies based on booming economies and their high demand to satisfy the growth. The publication states that countries with a state capitalism have direct access to these relevant minerals and metals neither through their state-owned enterprises in their own economies nor through strategic foreign direct investments (FDI) in these elements by Sovereign Wealth Funds (SWFs) or state-owned enterprises, too. The results of the survey show that these economies are going to have or already have an advantage attributable to this behaviour and that the European Union (EU) missed this opportunity decades ago. Moreover does this way of political behaviour not coincide with the idea of a capitalist economic system, which is based on a free and fair trade. Finally, the EU seems to cooperate in this issue less than they should or might be able to. Indications were found related to the Europe 2020 strategy that the EU could overcome this weakness.

Key words

Sovereign Wealth Funds, global shift, foreign exchange reserves, investments, Europe 2020 strategy, natural resources, minerals and metals, state capitalism, foreign direct investments, exchange reserves, emerging markets, developing and transition economies, developed economies, capitalist system, socialist system

CONTENT

LIST OF TABLES

LIST OF ABBREVIATIONS

BDI	Bundesverband der Deutschen Industrie e.V.
	engl.: The voice of German Industry (Representation of interests)
BP	British Petroleum
BRIC	Acronym for the countries Brazil, Russian Federation, India and China
CARG	Compound annual growth rate
CIA	Central Intelligence Agency
CIBUL	Centre for International Business at the University of Leeds
EU	European Union
EUSWF	European Union Sovereign Wealth Funds
FDI	Foreign direct investments
GAAP	Generally accepted accounting principles
GDP	Gross domestic product
IMF	International Monetary Fund
IWG	The International Working Group of Sovereign Wealth Funds
MNC	Multinational corporations
M&A	Mergers & acquisitions
OECD	Organisation for Economic Co-operation and Development
Q	Question
RMI	Raw Material Initiative
SWF	Sovereign Wealth Funds
TNC	Transnational Corporation
UAE	United Arab Emirates
UK	United Kingdom
UN	United Nations
US	United States
USA	United States of America
WTO	World Trade Organization
σ	Sigma, engl.: Standard deviation

1 Introduction

Global demographic developments are one of the greatest challenges of our century. In the twentieth century, the earth's population grew more quickly than ever before (Robert Bosch 2011). Regarding the Robert Bosch Global Megatrends study (2011) demographic change is one of the three major global megatrends. Other challenges for the future are accelerated globalization and scarcity of natural resources based on increasing demand for those resources through economic and population growth (Hajkowicz and Moody 2010). The publication will carve out how these challenges are interrelated and what national governments and the European Union (EU) should do to manage the challenges of scarcity of natural resources. This becomes obvious especially in a rough environment where certain governments use their geopolitical power to control access to raw materials. This was for example the case when China imposed export restrictions on various rare earths and other raw materials which were not in line with the World Trade Organization (WTO) rules (World Trade Organization 2011). In this context the phenomenon of Sovereign Wealth Funds (SWF) will be discussed and how SWFs lead to global challenges through long-term investing and how they could be a possible solution for the EU to overcome the scarcity of natural resources.

1.1 The world's need for energy and the war of natural raw material

During the past fifty years a plethora of natural resources crisis has attracted public, political and academic attention (Rees 1990, p. XIV). Natural resources should be considered as a gift of nature — a product of biological, ecological or geological processing. Natural resources are classified as non-renewable (stock) and renewable (flow). Figure 1 provides an overview of existing natural resources.

Stock			Flow	
Consumed by use	*Theoretically recoverable*	*Recyclable*	*Critical zone*	*Noncritical zone*
Oil	All elemental minerals	Metallic minerals	Fish	Solar energy
Gas			Forests	Tides
Coal			Animals	Wind
			Soil	Waves
			Water in aquifers	Water
				Air

Flow resources used to extinction

Critical zone resources become stock once regenerative capacity is exceeded

Figure 1: A basic classification of resources: Stock vs. Flow
[Generic deductive approach (Rees 1990)]

"Natural resources are not restricted to direct material inputs to economic life. They include a vast range of economic system services that are not directly consumed by use, but which are necessary for economic production and/or the maintenance of life" (Bridge 2009, p. 261). The focus of this publication is based on stock resources, specifically minerals and metals. Both natural resources are measured by their scarcity.

In explaining the matter of scarcity Bridge (2009) refers to the relational approach of the human geographers. This approach describes the scarcity of natural resources not only as a limitation due to a physical limit but also due to economic conditions. Two different versions of the relational approach can be distinguished: a 'weak' and a 'strong' version. The weak version states that there is hardly a physical limit to the availability of natural resources and therefore it is understood as a function of price and knowledge. The latter version refers to the technological changes which might reduce costs for recovering those resources. The strong version considers the societal inequality and reasons that scarcity is "an economic rather than a physical condition" (Bridge 2009, p. 264). Therefore, the availability is coordinated by wealth and power. Nevertheless, both versions coincide on the underlying assumption that the supply and demand for natural resources determines the price.

Regarding the United Nations' (UN) World Urbanization Prospects (United Nations 2010b) the world population will increase by 2.3 billion within the next four decades, from 6.8 billion in 2009 to 9.1 billion in 2050. This demographic change results among others in growing urbanization (United Nations 2010b, p. 1). This constant growth in urbanization is expected to result in a stronger demand for natural resources (Huang, Yeh and Chang 2010, p. 136). Developing countries play a critical role in these extensive discussions on population growth and urbanization (Huang, Yeh and Chang 2010, p. 136). Particularly Asia is of crucial importance due to the fact that most of the emerging markets are located in the Asian region, such as China, India and Vietnam. Their impact on the world is analysed in chapter 2.1.

Country-level analysis for the world's two population-richest countries China and India figure out that the demand for natural resources is outstripping the supply. Shen (2005, p. 287) mentioned that "China will inevitably face a long shortage of resources." China cannot meet its supply and demand for major natural resources to satisfy its growing industrialization and modernization. Gupta, Tuli and Verma (2005) mentioned India's growing need for energy. Today, India ranks as worldwide number five in terms of energy consumption. Economic growth and increasing incomes are pushing the demand and lead to the point that India will pass Japan as the world's number four. This leads to increasing and variable prices for natural resources (Gupta, Tuli and Verma 2005). Figure 2 illustrates the increasing demand for China and India.

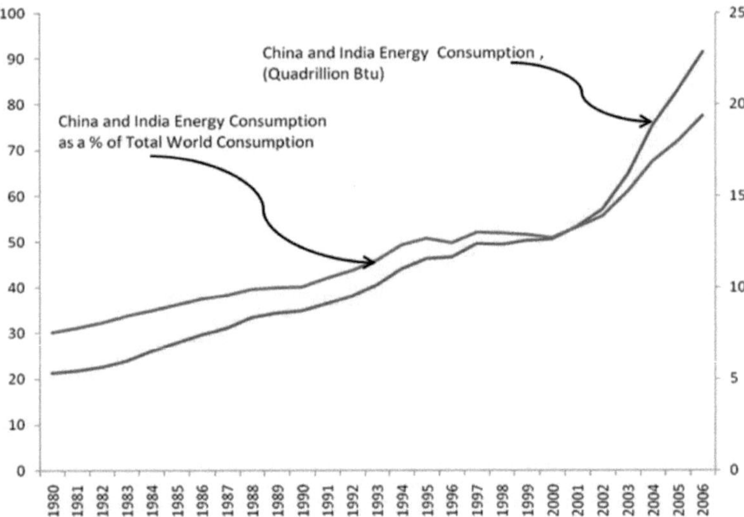

Figure 2: China and India are the world's leading energy consumers
(Bressand et al. 2007, p. 73)

This development leads to increasing stock prices induced by the imbalance of buyer (demand) and seller (supply) behaviour. It might occur that buyers are more anxious to buy than sellers are to sell, and vice versa (Frazier, Coyne and Witter 2002). There is a positive correlation between the increasing demand for natural resources especially for metals and minerals and the stock prices over the last years. Figure 3 demonstrates this development based on the World Bank Commodity Index.

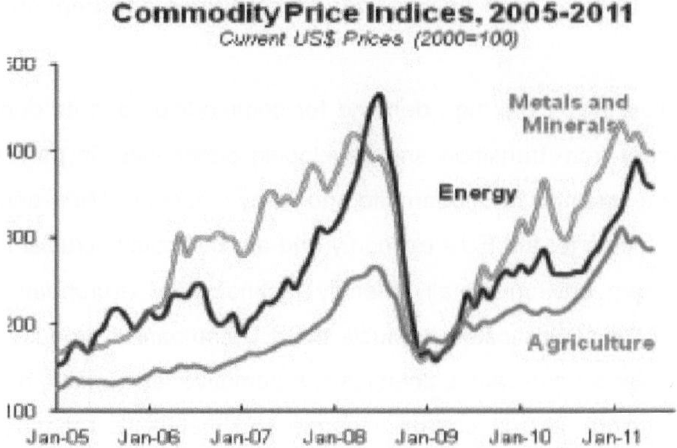

Figure 3: Commodity Price Indices, 2005 – 2011 (World Bank 2011)

As mentioned above, the demographic development which results in increased demand for natural resources has "significantly tightened the links between the world growth and commodity prices because growth has become more commodity-intensive, and the world commodity supply curve is becoming increasingly less elastic" (López 2010). Figure 4 illustrates these links and the effect for the price elastic.

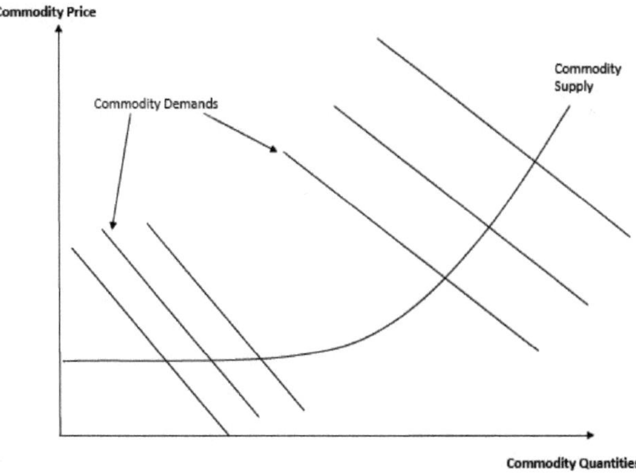

Figure 4: Commodity price elastic in past and present (López 2010)

1.2 European Union's high demand for commodities and dependency on imports

This chapter illustrates EU's high demand for commodities and its dependency on imports especially from transition and developing economies. In particular, certain commodities are essential for modern life and many industries. "Non-energy raw materials are vital inputs for the EU's economy and are particularly crucial for the development of modern environmentally friendly technologies" (European Commission 2008). Many of the sophisticated products that EU companies produce in particular industries like telecommunication, chemicals, automotive, aerospace, machinery and other hi-tech sectors rely on certain minerals and metals (European Commission 2011b). In general, the EU must import nearly all of these minerals and metals because its domestic production is limited to about 3 percent of world production (European Commission 2011b). Figure 5 shows the import rate of specific metals and minerals in the EU.

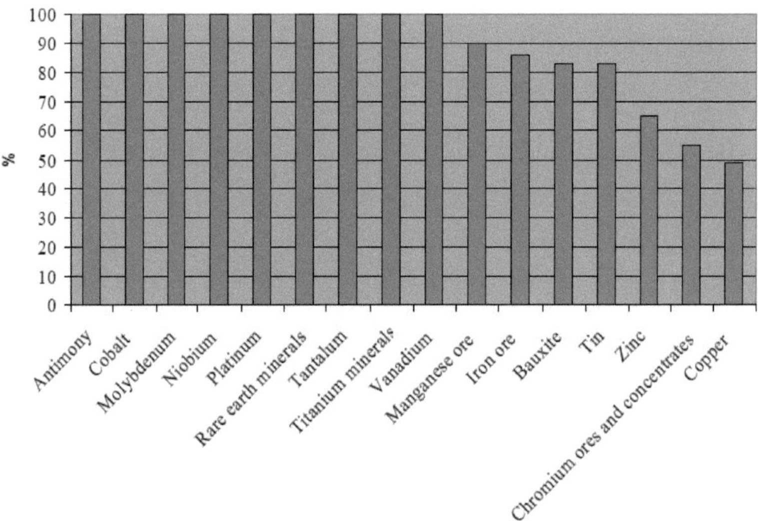

Figure 5: Metal concentrates and ores — net imports as percent of apparent consumption (European Commission 2008, p. 4)

EU's dependency on imports leads to risk — especially because of the large technology sector. The main risk would be that commodities cannot be imported, but also increasing demand and prices impose a risk on the EU, especially if production prices explode and product prices are not competitive with international markets. The import risk is driven by the fact that most of the importing countries are transition and developing economies use barriers for export and import to achieve advantages (see chapter 2.3). Figure 6 generally illustrates that the EU depends on the supply of other countries.

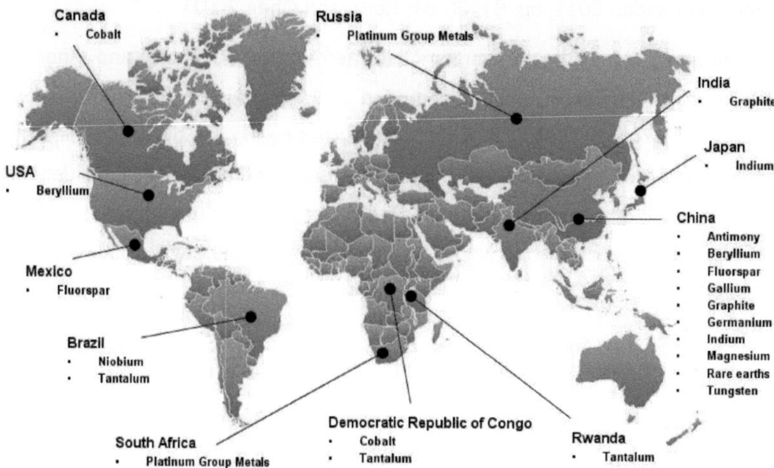

Figure 6: Production concentration of critical raw mineral materials
(European Commission 2011a)

The price and demand relation is driven by two factors, mainly by the increasing demand through growing population and also through envisioning environmental-friendly technologies. Selected minerals and metals which are important and relevant for the above mentioned EU industries are:

- Lithium is strongly driven by the consumer electronic, telecommunication and automotive sector due to its use in batteries because rechargeable lithium batteries are used in laptops, mobile phones and e-cars.

- Gallium is a highly demanded element for consumer goods, industrial equipment, telecommunication and medical equipment based on the fact that it is used for semiconductors and optoelectronic devices like light-emitting diodes, laser diodes, photo cameras and solar cells.

- Copper is extensively used for electrical applications and construction, accounting for about 33 percent each of total copper usage but also in (Berry and Chen 2001) air-conditioning systems. In general, copper is one of the elements which has strongly increased through new technologies (David Folkerts-Landau 2011, pp. 61, 80-81; Berry and Chen 2001).

EU telecommunication, chemicals, automotive, aerospace, machinery and other hi-tech sectors which provide a total value added of 1,324 billion Euros and employment for around 30 million people is directly influenced by the use of certain minerals and metals. But there are also a lot of different sectors which are indirectly influenced by the development of these metals and minerals. For example: In Germany, one out of seven jobs depends on the automotive sector — one of the key industries of the country (Oberthür 2011, p. 1; Tajani 2011, pp. 1-4).

1.3　The power of Sovereign Wealth Funds

Over the last years, the role of Sovereign Wealth Funds (SWFs) in the global financial system has increased (Schoar and Koerner 2010, p. 2). Regarding Clark & Monk (2010, p. 1) SWFs are "[...] representatives of nation-states in global financial markets, [...] share a common form and many functions." This publication explores how SWFs can confront global challenges through long-term investing and how they could be a solution for the EU to overcome the scarcity of natural resources. In general, SWFs are large pools of government-owned funds that are invested as a whole or in part outside their home country (Truman 2010, p. IX). As mentioned above, SWFs are not a new phenomenon (Griffith-Jones and Ocampo 2010), but their remarkable growing in number and size is impressive (United States Congress House of Representatives 2008). The assets under management of these funds are estimated to reach $4.0 trillion in 2011 — over the past decades, they have continually grown from $500 billion in 1990 to the actual value and will increase significantly within the next years (Kotter and Lel 2011, p. 1). The expected growth in SWFs assets under management is $10 trillion till 2020 (Bolton and Samama 2010, p. 14). Regarding Clark & Monk (2010, p. 1) "one of which sees SWFs becoming financial goliaths dominating global markets, while the other sees SWFs morphing into nation-state development institutions that intermediate between financial markets and the long-term commitments of the nation-state sponsors." Whatever happens in the long term SWFs have developed to become an important investor in global capital markets (Laeven 2010, p. 1). At this point it is irrelevant whether the SWFs are funded by a government based on a capitalist or socialist system (Avendaño and Santiso 2010). Chapter 2.2 will provide more details concerning the universe of SWFs.

1.4 Guideline to answer the research question and objectives

The overall research question of the publication is **"Strategic SWF investments as a possible solution in the war of resources"**: Is a strategic SWF investment an adequate instrument for national governments to secure access to critical raw material and energy inputs?

This research question covers several research objectives which have been developed to ensure that the question will be answered appropriately:

- Why is there a need for some countries to secure raw material and energy inputs?
- Do developing and transition economies take advantage of state-owned investments?
- Has the European Union a need to secure access to critical natural resources?
- Is a European Union Sovereign Wealth Fund (EUSWF) an adequate instrument to achieve this goal?

The aim of the publication is to create awareness that the world faces a scarcity of natural resources and to analyse the reasons for this challenge. The publication is also going to specify possible solutions as well as evaluate and develop one possible solution for the war of resources.

To answer the research question mentioned above the publication follows a six chapter structure. The introduction covered the ground of the topic by introducing the most important facts and the central issues of the main challenges in the twenty-first century. Therefore, it explained the most important facts about development of scarcity of natural resources, illustrated the EU's and Germany's high demand for commodities and introduced an SWF as a possible solution.

One of the main parts of the publication is the literature review. It analyses the current state of debate and highlights new aspects. For this purpose, the literature review broaches the issue of shift in global economic power and explains SWFs and the state capitalism's relevance and dependency on natural-resources management in developed countries, supplemented by the issues of the responsibilities of governments or market powers.

Chapter 3 describes and justifies the choice of the case study methodology and the research strategy supported by current literature to examine the reasons for the scarcity of natural resources and analyse SWFs as the possible problem solver. The developed results will be illustrated in chapter 4 of this publication. Chapter 5 discusses the results and specific implications for the EU. It also illustrates the main limitations with regard to the research results and proposes further fields of research to be able to appraise the gained findings and draw definite conclusions. A conclusion in chapter 6 summarizes the main issues and completes the publication.

2 Literature Review

After introducing the topic and highlighting its overall importance this chapter is focusing on the current development by providing a review of the existing literature. The geographical location of natural resources as well as the connection between natural resources and the shift of global economic power is illustrated. Furthermore, the phenomena of SWF and the state capitalism, the need to secure access to natural resources and the current activities of the EU are explained. Both aspects underline that access to and control of natural resources can primarily be considered as an issue of national resources security and geopolitical power (Bridge 2009, p. 265).

2.1 Shift of global economic power

There is a shift of global economic activity from developed to developing economies accompanied by growth in the number of consumers in emerging markets (Dye and Stephenson 2010, p. 1). The shift reflects the economic laws of gravity. Meaning that in "a world where ideas can flow freely and countries are at different stages in adopting modern modes of production, communication and distribution, less developed nations should grow more rapidly" (Byran 2010, p. 3). Based on Adam Smith's theory 'law of one price' the most important input factors for production are commodities, capital and labour. In a fully informed market all items should be available for the same price[1] (Byran 2010, p. 7).

As early as 2003, Goldman Sachs mentioned in its report (Wilson and Purushothaman 2003, p. 3) 'Dreaming with BRICs: The Path to 2050' the impressive growth in the emerging markets. The report focused on the BRIC[2] economies which have the potential of an average real gross domestic product (GDP) growth of 4 to 8

---

[1] In a fully informed market all items should be available for the same price. Also, freely traded foreign exchange and most instruments traded in the capital market should be available for every market participant. However, this law does not apply for labour, which is the fundamental structural issue the global economy faces. BYRAN, L. 2010. Globalization's critical imbalance. *McKinsey Quarterly,* (June).

[2] The acronym BRIC stands for the economies with the largest potential: Brazil, Russia, India and China.

percent per year till 2025. The US and the EU only had a projected real GDP[3] growth of 2 to 2.5 percent per year, which decelerated to 1 to 1.5 percent till 2025. The enormous real GDP growth is also reflected in the increasing exchange reserves. Brazil increased its exchange reserves from 2001 to 2011 from $38 billion to $330 billion. In the same period the other BRIC countries also increased their exchange reserves: Russian Federation from $36 billion to $521 billion, China from $286[4] billion to $2,876[5] billion and India from $8 billion to $311 billion. The BRIC economies hold nearly 40 percent of the total $9.6 trillion foreign exchange holding (International Monetary Fund 2011b; Reserve Bank of India 2011; Bank of Russia 2011; Central Intelligence Agency (CIA) 2011). The afore mentioned shift illustrated by the example of the BRIC economies is not just adduced by the GDP growth rate but also as mentioned in Chapter 1.1 by the growing population rate, which make the BRIC states one of the largest economies of consumption with a world population share of 40 percent[6].

In his study 'How solid are the BRICs?' Jim O'Neill et al. (2005) focused on other emerging markets naming them 'Next Eleven' or 'N-11'[7]. This study identified the following eleven countries as emerging: Bangladesh, Egypt, Indonesia, Iraq, South Korea, Mexico, Nigeria, Pakistan, the Philippines, Turkey and Vietnam[8]. Mexico and South Korea are members of the OECD but an official definition of developed and

---

[3] Own calculation based on Wilson & Purushothaman WILSON, D. and R. PURUSHOTHAMAN. 2003. Dreaming with BRICs: The Path to 2050. *Goldman Sachs — Global Economics,* **Paper No. 99**.

[4] Published by the School of Finance Renmin University of China ZHAO, X. and S. ZHANG. 2006. *Report on China's Foreign Exchange Reserves*. Beijing: School of Finance Renmin University of China.

[5] Estimation from the Central Intelligence Agency (CIA): Date: December 31st, 2010 CENTRAL INTELLIGENCE AGENCY (CIA). 2011. *The World Factbook — Country Comparison: Reserves of foreign exchange and gold* [online]. [Accessed July 14th, 2011]. Available from:
https://www.cia.gov/library/publications/the-world-factbook/rankorder/2188rank.html.

[6] The BRIC countries are therefore larger than the G6. The G6 consist of Germany, US, Japan, UK, France and Italy. G6 are the largest six among the G7 with a real GDP growth of over $1000 billion (WILSON, D. and R. PURUSHOTHAMAN. 2003. Dreaming with BRICs: The Path to 2050. *Goldman Sachs — Global Economics,* **Paper No. 99**.

[7] Jim O'Neill is Head of Global Economic Research of Goldman Sachs and creator of the acronym BRIC GOLDMAN SACHS. 2008. *Interview with Jim O'Neill* [online]. [Accessed July 10th, 2011]. Available from: http://www2.goldmansachs.com/ideas/brics/index.html.

[8] Mexico and South Korea are members of the OECD but an official definition of developed and developing or emerging markets does not exist.

developing or emerging markets does not exist (O'Neill *et al.* 2005). Based on the projection the 'Next Eleven' have the potential to belong to the world's twenty largest national economies. Mexico and South Korea even have the potential to be on the same level with the BRIC economies. The study 'How solid are the BRICs?' reappraised the projections of the BRIC economies. The result was that all BRIC economies are above the projected real GDP growth rates.

The mentioned studies are only pars pro toto to illustrate the shift of the global economy. Both studies only analysed economies with a significant population which have the potential for a global impact[9]. The following projections reinforce the notion that by 2025 and especially by 2050, different economies than today will be the largest in US dollar terms. Figure 7 shows the largest economies of the future:

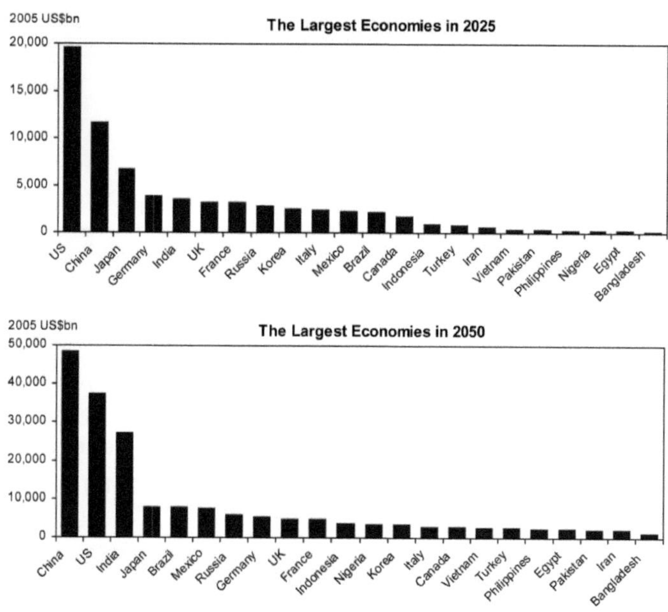

Figure 7: The Largest Economies (O'Neill *et al.* 2005)

---

[9] Due to this economies like Hong Kong are not mentioned in these studies although they show enormous GDP growth rates.

However, other studies analysed the development of the shifts in global economic power. Farrel (2007, p. 62) also expected that within the next years one-third of global economic growth will be generated in the emerging countries. The McKinsey Global Survey's[10] (2010) results underline that not only economists share the view of the global economy shift but also executives. The survey reports that 40 percent of executives at companies' headquarters in developed economies expect that a quarter or more of revenues come from emerging markets in the next five years.

Figure 8 illustrates the world's distribution of wealth and power. With reference to Bridge (2009, p. 263) wealth is characterised by access to natural resources. Therefore, wealth and power are positively correlated.

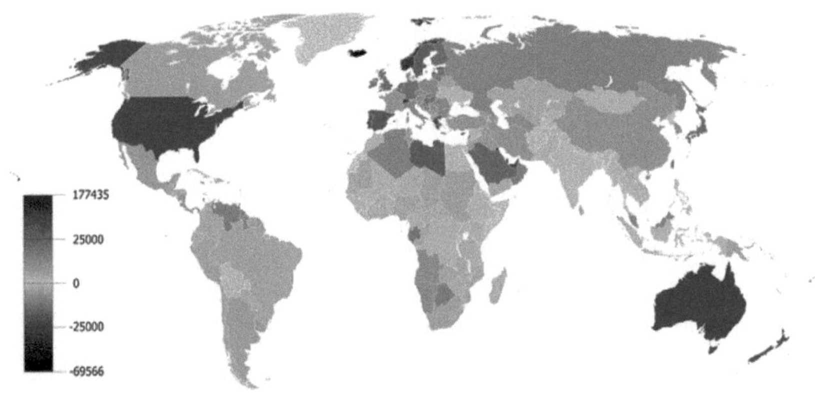

Figure 8: World's wealth and power based on foreign currency reserves and gold minus external debt (O'Neill *et al.* 2005; Haisenko 2010)

---

[10] The online survey generated responses from 1.416 executives around the world, representing the full range of industries, regions, functional specialties and seniority.

2.2 The universe of Sovereign Wealth Funds

The International Monetary Fund (IMF) and Financial Committee[11] mentioned SWFs as institutional investors and important participants in the international monetary and financial system (Suwaidi and Caruana 2008). Furthermore, SWFs are funded by the state governments and are primarily founded in developing and transnational countries and the shift of global wealth and power is reflected in the activities and assets under management of the SWFs. This chapter gives an overview of the purpose of SWFs based on their nature and the 'non-transparency' universe in which they engage (Kotter and Lel 2011).

2.2.1 Definition and history

There is not a general or clear definition of SWFs wherefore a dissociation of different funds between SWFs, pension funds and investment funds is complicated. The identification of a fund, especially of SWFs, is a problem because SWFs do not have separate legal forms and are deployed as state-owned enterprises, central banks or investment funds (Beck and Fidora 2008, p. 6). In the following, three key elements for identification are mentioned:

1. SWFs are owned by the general government or are under the direct control of the government.

2. SWFs are funded by the public sector. Typically, the money originates from the budget surplus but also from the monetary and reserve exchanges. However, the money from the SWFs is managed independently from the money and exchange reserves.

3. SWFs do not or only have small indebtedness and are long-term investors. (Kern 2007a, p. 3; Beck and Fidora 2008, p. 6)

However, SWFs have a different history of origins. The relevance within the country and the purpose depends on the nature of its origins. SWFs could be categorized by

---

[11] The IMFC is a committee of the Board of Governors of the International Monetary Fund (IMF), comprising representatives — typically ministers of finance and central bank governors — of all 185 IMF member countries.

their purpose into three types. These three types arise from three different time phases.

The first SWF was founded by Kuwait in 1953 which is nowadays the world's fourth largest SWF (Beck and Fidora 2008). This one belongs to the first type and started the first phase. Jen (2007, p. 1) named the SWFs of the first type **Stabilization Funds** which have the purpose to reduce or to eliminate economic fluctuation in the fiscal policy. Examples are the oil producing countries or export orientated countries like Singapore which try to compensate national budget revenues in times of decreasing oil prices by using the revenues from the Stabilization Fund SWFs. The establishing wave started in the seventies with the beginning of the first oil crisis in 1973 (Kern 2007b).

The second phase started in the nineties with the increasing importance of sustainability thinking. The second type of SWFs which were established in this phase are called **Generation Funds or Wealth Funds**. Those manage the assets of the current revenues and prorate the assets to the future generation of the countries. Normally, this happens in countries which participate in the oil wealth and which are aware of the fact that their oil wealth is endless (Jen 2007, p. 1; Kern 2007b, p. 3).

The third phase started at the beginning of the twenty-first century. The SWFs of type three are the **Exchange Funds** which receive their assets from the exchange reserves. Especially emerging countries like China and the Russian Federation, which generated large exchange reserves, transfer these into SWFs[12]. These SWFs are funds of the superlative with enormous assets under management.

Since the establishing of the first SWFs in 1953 nowadays there are between 31 and 50 SWFs. Table 1 provides a current and extensive overview of existing SWFs:

---

[12] Based on the nature of type three the Japanese Liberal Democratic Party is planning to establish an SWF (KIKUCHI, M. and H. NAGAYOSHI. 2008. LDP's SWF concept. *Merrill Lynch — Japan Strategy Memo*).

Table 1: Worldwide overview of SWFs (Author's own[13])

No.	Country	Name of Fund	Establishment	Source	Volume (bn.USD)
1	UAE (Abu Dhabi)	Abu Dhabi Investment Authority	1976	Oil	875
2	Norway	Government Pension Fund	1990	Oil	394
3	Saudi Arabia	Saudi Arabian Monetary Agency	1952	Oil	371
4	Singapore	Government of Singapore Invest. Corporation	1981	Surplus	330
5	China	SAFE Investment Company	1997	Exchange res	312
6	Kuwait	Kuwait Investment Authority	1953	Oil	265
7	China	China Investment Corporation	2007	Exchange res	200
8	HongKong	Hong Kong Monetary Authority	1993	Exchange rer.	173
9	Russia	National Welfare Fund	2004	Oil	163
10	Singapore	Temasek Holdings	1974	Surplus	134
11	UAE (Dubai)	Investment Corporation of Dubai	2006	Oil	82-150*
12	Australia	Future Fund	2004	Surplus	64
13	Qatar	Qatar Investment Authority	2003	Oil	60
14	Lybia	Libyan Investment Authority	2006	Oil	50
15	Alergia	Revenue Regulation Fund	2000	Oil	47
16	Kazakhstan	Kazakhstan National Fund	2000	Surplus	38
17	South Korea	Korea Investment Corporation	2005	Surplus	30
18	Brunei	Brunei Investment Agency	1983	Oil	30
19	Malysia	Khazanah Nasional	1993	Surplus	26
20	Chile	Pension Reserve and Social Stabilization Fund.	1985	Oil	16
21	Taiwan	National Stabilisation Fund	2000	Surplus	15
22	New Zealand	New Zealand Superannuation Fund	2003	Surplus	15
23	Bahrain	Bahrain Mumtalakat Holding Company	2006	Oil	14
24	Iran	Oil Stabilisation Fund	1998	Oil	13
25	Oman	State General Reserve Fund	1980	Oil	13
26	Nigeria	Nigeria - Excess Crude Account	2004	Oil	11
27	Azerbaijan	State Oil Fund	1999	Oil	10
28	Botswana	Pula Fund	1966	Surplus	7
29	East Timor	Timor-Leste Petroleum Fund	2005	Oil	3
30	Vietnam	State Capital Investment Corporation	2005	Surplus	2
31	UAE (Ras Al Khaimah)	RAK Investment Authority	2004	Oil	1
32	Venezuela	FIEM - Macroeconomic Stabilization Fund	1998	Oil	0,8
33	Kiribati	Revenue Equalization Reserve Fund	1956	Surplus	0,5
34	Trinidad & Tobago	Heritage and Stabilization Fund	2000	Oil	0,5
35	Mauritania	National Fund for Hydrocarbon Reserves	2006	Oil	0,3
36	Angola	Reserve Fund for Oil	2004	Oil	0,2
I	UAE	Emirates Investment Authority	2008	Oil	n.a.
	Total				**3684,3**
SWF extends by the Canadian Provinces and American Federalstates					
A	Canada	Alberta's Heritage Fund	1976	Oil	17
B	USA	Alaska Permanent Fund	1976	Oil	40
C	USA	Alabama Trust Fund	1986	Oil	3,1
D	USA	New Mexico State Investment Office Trust	1958	Surplus	16
F	USA	Permanent Wyoming Mineral Trust Fund	1974	Oil	3,9
	Total				**3764,3**
Countries which planning to establish SWF					
A	Brazil	---		Exchange res	20
B	Japan	---		Exchange res	n.a.
C	India	---		Exchange res	n.a.
D	Bolivia	---		Oil	n.a.
E	Thailand	---		Surplus	n.a.

* not part of the total volume

---

[13] The volume and names of the SWFs are primarily based on the SWF Institute but also on homepages or annual reports.

2.2.2 Power of SWFs and investment strategy

The majority of the SWFs are located in Asia and the Middle Eastern region. Based on their sources SWFs are established typically in these regions. Figure 9 provides an overview of SWFs worldwide.

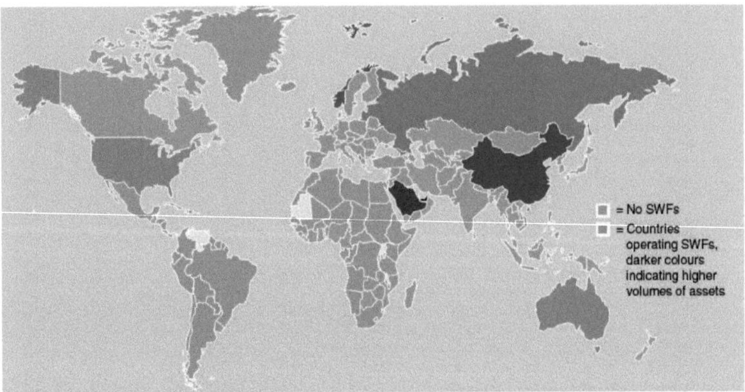

Figure 9: Worldwide distribution of SWFs and their volume (Kern 2007a)

These SWFs belong to the largest of the world. The SWFs from these regions are holding around 80 percent of all assets (Bolton and Samama 2010, p. 6). It is also expected that SWFs are growing over time in absolute and relative terms. This reflects the large balance of payment surplus in the emerging countries with are rich on resources and the increasing exchange reserves which are transferred into SWFs. In 2000, the global exchange reserves had an amount of $1.9 trillion and increased up to around $9.2 trillion in 2010 driven by the developing and transition economies. This is a factor of 4.7 within a decade. (International Monetary Fund 2011a, pp. 8-9) The compound annual growth rate is 23.97 percent for the transition and developing economies and 9.77 percent for developed economies. An own estimation with the same annual growth rates led to the result that the global exchange reserves will grow up to over $60 trillion in 2020. This development is illustrated in Figure 10.

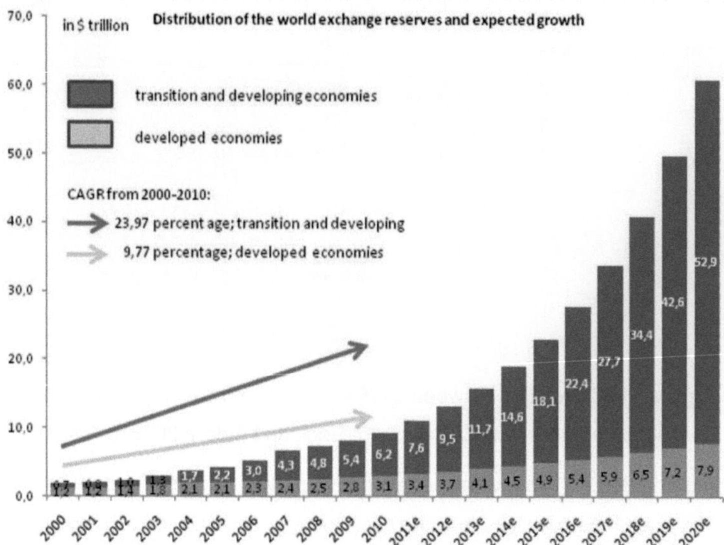

Figure 10: Global foreign exchange reserves outvalue the $9 trillion
(Author's own based on International Monetary Fund 2011a, pp. 8-9)

However, there is an unproportional correlation between the total growth and the re-
gional distribution. The developing and transition economies are driving the growth
especially through the Asian economies — in particular China with $2,876 billion
(Beck and Fidora 2008, p. 8; Bolton and Samama 2010, p. 15). These economies
increase the percentage of total exchange reserves from 37 percent in 2000 to 66
percent in 2010 a. In 2020 the percentage of total exchange reserves will be 87 percent.

Figure 11 shows that there is a strong negative correlation between exchange reserves and SWFs' volume. Economies with exchange funds still hold large exchange
reserves.

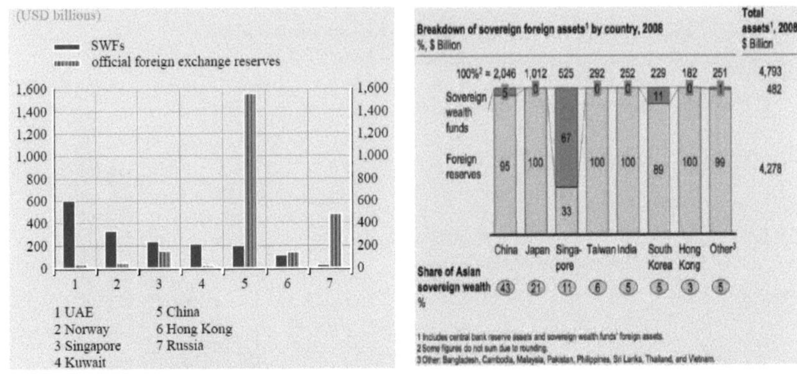

Figure 11: Correlation between SWF's volume and exchange reserves
(Bolton and Samama 2010, p. 15; Beck and Fidora 2008, p. 23)

Regarding chapter 2.1 'Shift of global economic power' in combination with the idea of growing exchange reserves and the fact that the demand for commodities is increasing worldwide, also for oil prices (United States Congress House of Representatives 2008), it becomes obvious that the expected growth of SWF's amount of assets from $4 trillion to $10 trillion is realistic (Bolton and Samama 2010).

Based on their enormous growth SWFs have to invest in foreign direct investments (FDI) (Farrel *et al.* 2007, pp. 63-64). On the one hand side, the home equity for the held assets is not large enough and they would risk inflation due to the fact that they give too much liquidity to the home economy. On the other hand side, asset allocation is essential based on the theory of risk diversification. The main question is about their investment objective: whether it is economically or a politically motivated. In terms of **Stabilization Funds** and **Generation Funds** which have already existed for a while since their investment strategy is known. Reports show that they have an asset allocation between 40 — 60 percent in fixed income and vice versa in equity to follow an economic motive (Farrel *et al.* 2007, p. 53; Norges Bank Investment Management 2011). This motive is also evidenced through former investments especially during the financial crisis when SWFs invested more than $60 billion in US and European banks, accounting for two thirds of the total amount invested (Kern 2008). Overall, it is not clear whether SWFs' investment, especially **Exchange Funds,** is based on financial or political objectives (Kotter and Lel 2011). Avendaño & Santiso

20

(2010, p. 3) says that "very little is known about SWFs [...] but there is a difference between autocratic, imperfect democracy regimes and democratic." Regarding the hearing of SWF experts at the United States Congress House of Representatives (United States Congress House of Representatives 2008, p. 2) SWFs, based on their nature, "should always be viewed as maximizing their nation's strategy interests." This fact is relevant when discussing countries like the Russian Federation and China. Their security and economic interests are not always consistent with those of the EU or the US (United States Congress House of Representatives 2008).

2.2.3 Transparency

The fear that SWFs are "created by the general government for macroeconomic purposes [...]" (Suwaidi and Caruana 2008, p. 3) and the fact that SWFs are large enough to be systemically significant and have the potential to create chaos in the markets and take an important role in the war of resources (United States Congress House of Representatives 2008) is supported and driven by the low level of transparency.

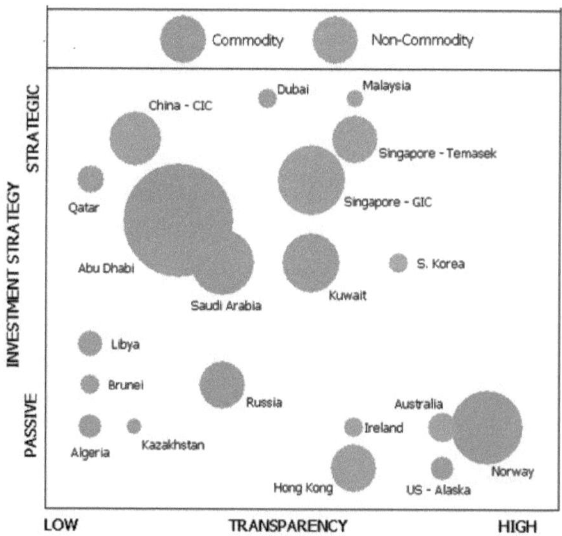

Figure 12: Investment strategy and transparency of SWFs (SWF Institute 2008)

It seems to be apparent that there is a need for more transparency to make sure that SWFs are invested more beneficially rather than critical into international markets. In October 2006, the IMF endorsed the generally accepted principles and practices (GAAP) also known as 'The Santiago Principles' to assure that SWF investments are made on an economic and financial basis (Suwaidi and Caruana 2008, pp. 1-11; Bolton and Samama 2010, p. 21). The goals of the GAAP are (Suwaidi and Caruana 2008, p.4):

- To help maintain a stable global financial system and free flow of capital and investment;

- To comply with all applicable regulatory and disclosure requirements in the countries in which they invest;

- To invest on the basis of economic and financial risk and return-related considerations; and

- To have in place a transparent and sound governance structure that provides for adequate operational controls, risk management, and accountability.

The purpose of the GAAP is to support the institutional framework, governance and investment operations of SWFs that are guided by their policy purpose and objectives and that are consistent with a sound macroeconomic policy framework. (Suwaidi and Caruana 2008, p 4)

The objective is that SWFs demonstrate "a clear willingness to show a real independence from the governments" (Bolton and Samama 2010, p. 21). A detailed guideline of 'The Santiago Principles' is provided in the appendix 4.

Based on the facts of non-transparency, limited information, problem of definition and SWFs in general have been involved in a large share of FDI flows (Gugler 2010). The state capitalism based on more information will be analysed in chapter 2.3.

2.3 State capitalism's come of age

To refer to Wolnicki (2010, p. 480) "the term 'state capitalism' was used by Marxists and heterodox economists to describe a society where the productive forces are owned and run by the state in a capitalist way."

2.3.1 A rising outward FDI from transition and developing economies

As mentioned in chapter 2.1 and 2.1 there is a growing population and a rapid economic growth in the emerging, developing and transition economies. This leads to larger consumption but also to larger investment based on an accumulation of capital (Dye and Stephenson 2010, p. 2; United Nations 2010a). Based on the World Investment Report 2010 (United Nations 2010a, p. 6) the share of developing and transition economies in global FDI outflows is on an all-time high. The largest economies in the developing and transition economies China and the Russian Federation are ranked under the top 20 investors of the world. Figure 13 illustrates this ranking:

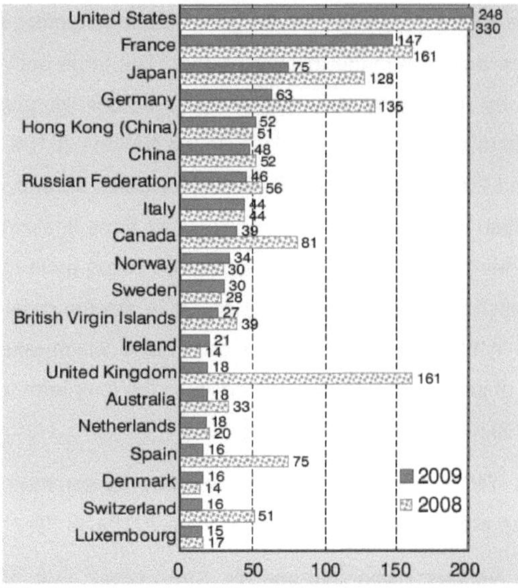

Figure 13: Global FDI outflows, top 20 home economies (United Nations 2010a, p. 6)

Transnational corporations (TNCs) of these economies, namely China and the Russian Federation, plus India and Brazil have turned into dynamic investors (United Nations 2010a). Figure 14 shows that in 2008, BRICs have invested more than $147 billion in outward foreign direct investments — almost 9 percent of the worldwide outflows.

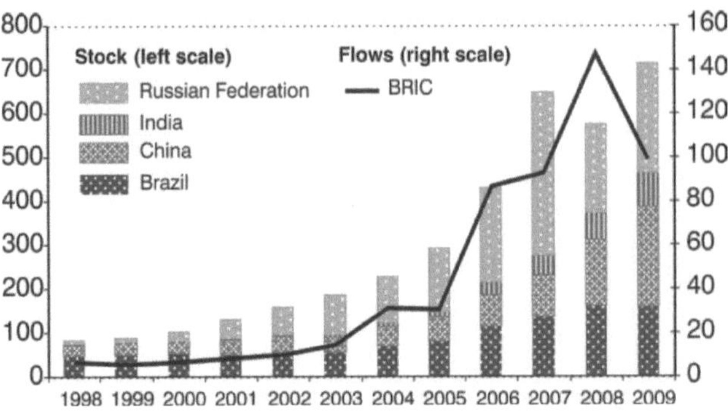

Figure 14: Outward FDI flows and stocks from BRIC (United Nations 2010a, p. 7)

After an overall decrease in FDI due to the global economic crisis in 2009, they will again increase their activities in the following years. The large outflows of FDI of the BRIC are driven by increasing volumes of cross-border mergers & acquisitions (M&As). The World Investment Report 2010 (United Nations 2010a, p. 7) reports that "between 2000 and 2009, Indian firms finalized 812 deals abroad, Chinese firms finalized 450, Brazilian firms finalized 190 and Russian firms finalized 436" and that a majority of these deals were valued at more than $1 billion even in 2010. This illustrates that multinational corporations (MNC) or TNCs are the most important global economic players in this growing FDI and globalization which takes advantages of global economies of scale to maximize profitability in the long term and the short term (Kirkland 2009, p. 2).

However, BRIC's TNCs have four specific features in common (United Nations 2010a, p. 7). These are listed below (United Nations 2010a, p. 7):

- They have various ownership-specific advantages that allow them to be competitive in foreign markets as well as in their own markets. If they invested in organizations abroad they have elicited portfolios of local assets as increasingly important sources of their international competitiveness.

- They still have an affinity to expand in their own region especially in those countries with intercultural connections. However, a growing number of TNCs has risked discovering new markets and resources

- A large number of BRICs TNCs have become real global players in terms of global brand names, management skills and competitive business models.

- They are often motivated by strategic considerations rather than by short-term profitability. This fact reflects the role of state-owned enterprises in the outward FDI of the group.

With reference to the last point fast-growing Asian economies "[...] routinely endeavoured to shape economic outcomes by developing and implementing industrial policy, managing exchange rates, deploying markets, and using state-owned assets" (Skilling 2009). Governmental support measures will and already did secure the rising outward FDI — especially in the BRIC economies.

2.3.2 Government as principal actor

Governments are the principal actors in economic activities. And especially governments in the Asian economies — except for India — already have a significant impact on their economies and that well in advance of the discussion about governments' involvements in economic activities (Skilling 2009, p. 2; Wolnicki 2010, p. 480). For the first time in the late 1960s when the expansion of MNCs started (Shemirani 2011, p. 5), politicians and academics have led this discussion and have used the word "state capitalism" for the first time when the members of the Organization of the Petroleum Exporting Countries (OPEC) agreed to reduce the oil production as an economic-political response to the United States' support of Israel in the Yom Kippur War (Bremmer 2009b, p. 5). However, today state-directed economic activities have a great impact on the globalization (Kirkland 2009, p. 2). This is underlined by a study from Dye & Stephenson (2010, p. 7) that says that a very high percentage of 64 percent characterizes the Chinese government as the principal actor in their country's economy (only 49 percent of the respondents in China shared this view).

The current development is best described by Shemirani (2011, p. 5): "Today, big government is back with a vengeance: not just as a brute fact, but as a vigorous ideology [...]. The world is seeing the rise of a new economic hybrid — what might be termed 'state capitalism.'" Bremmer (2009a, p. 4) explains state capitalism as "an economic system in which governments manipulate market outcomes for political purposes. Governments embrace state capitalism because it serves political as well as economic purposes — not only because it's the most efficient way of generating prosperity. It puts vast financial resources within the control of state officials, allowing them access to cash that helps safeguard their domestic political capital and, in many cases, increases their leverage on the international stage." In doing so governments have a set of tools:

- Government policies such as China's "go global" encourage domestic enterprises to invest globally, but also Brazil's, India's and the Russian Federation's statements to create global players through incentives or often called 'national champions' (United Nations 2010a, p. 7).

- Foreign exchange rates are adjusted, such as a liberalization in India or a fixed currency converter rate in China (Luedi 2008, p. 1).

- Investment vehicles hold and control financial and physical assets which are done by national oil corporations, state-owned enterprises, national champions and SWFs (Skilling 2009, p. 2; Bremmer 2009b). Furthermore, these vehicles could expand by transforming the ongoing accumulations of exchange reserves and balance surplus (Blessing 2007, p. 11). The BRIC are holding exchange reserves of nearly 40 percent and the Asian economies are holding two thirds of the total exchange reserves (see chapter 2.2 and figure 10).

- All tools are based on a business model given the friction between free-market and state-driven capitalism.

2.3.3 Geopolitical strategy

The state capitalism economies have a lot of specific natural resources under their control either in their own countries or in other countries through strategic investments driven by an economic or political policy and as shown by the examples in chapter 2.2 TNCs and SWFs used their state dominance to expand their business. That means that they also heavily invested in the oil market. The largest global players are state-owned TNCs. Furthermore, lot of Chinese TNCs and some Brazilian, Indian and Russian TNCs are also state-controlled. The large and transparent market for oil and gas companies will serve as **a good example**. Table 2 provides an overview based on those companies holding the largest reserves of oil and natural gas in terms of million barrels.

Table 2: Ranking by total reserves in oil and natural gas
(Petro Strategies Incorporation 2011)

1	Saudi Arabian Oil Company	Saudi Arabia	303,285	State-owned
2	National Iranian Oil Company	Iran	300,485	State-owned
3	Qatar General Petroleum Corporation	Qatar	169,959	State-owned
4	Iraq National Oil Company	Iraq	134,135	State-owned
5	Petroleos de Venezuela.S.A.	Venezuela	128,594	State-owned
6	Abu Dhabi National Oil Company	UAE	126,132	State-owned
7	Kuwait Petroleum Corporation	Kuwait	110,990	State-owned
8	Nigerian National Petroleum Corp.	Nigeria	67,671	State-owned
9	National Oil Company	Libya	50,028	State-owned
10	Sonatrach	Algeria	39,379	State-owned
11	Gazprom	Russian Federation	29,261	State-owned
12	OAO Rosneft	Russian Federation	21,805	State-owned
13	PetroChina Co. Ltd.	China	21,469	State-owned
14	Petronas	Malaysia	19,547	State-owned
15	OAO Lukoil	Russian Federation	15,720	State-owned
16	Egyptian General Petroleum Corp.	Egypt	13,700	State-owned
17	ExxonMobil Corporation	USA	13,318	Private
18	Petroleos Mexicanos	Mexico	13,198	State-owned
19	BP Corporation	UK	12,523	Private
20	Petroleo Brasilerio S.A.	Oman	10,628	State-owned
21	Chevron Corporation	USA	10,870	Private
22	Royal Dutch/Shell	Netherlands	10,767	Private

Well-known companies like Exxon Mobil, BP, Chevron and Shell only rank between places 17 to 22. The largest oil and gas companies in the world, measured by their reserves, are owned and operated by governments. The state-owned companies control more than 75 percent of the global oil and gas reserves and production. Private companies produce 10 percent of the total oil and gas and hold just 3 percent of these reserves. Also in other sectors of natural resources such as petrochemical, mining, iron, steel and minerals state-owned TNCs are global players with a monopoly or oligopoly position. Good examples are Angola's Endiama (diamonds), Azerbaijan's AzerEnerji (electricity generation), Kazakhstan's Kazatomprom (uranium) and Morocco's Office Chérifien des Phosphates. The private competitors have to compete with these state-owned TNCs because many governments are no longer satisfied with only regulating the market (Bremmer 2009b, pp. 2-3).

The mentioned economic growth accelerates the world's consumption of natural resources at an unpredicted rate (Bozon, Campbell and Lindstrand 2007, p. 49), especially in the developing and transition economies. Based on this the geopolitical strategy is to support national TNCs and to buy assets which will have positive spillover effects for the economic development to face the rising demand of natural resources and to win the war of resources (United States Congress House of Representatives 2008, p. 27). Regarding Luedi (2008, p. 76) this behaviour is maybe only one out of many globalization strategies. The following section shows some of the current activities of geopolitical strategy to reach for and get control of strategic assets. Resources-rich countries primarily based in Africa reviewed large foreign direct investments. Due to this 32 percent of Africa's GDP growth between 2000 and 2008 is based on natural resources and related governments spending (Leke *et al.* 2010). Natural resources like minerals, metals as well as oil have boosted Africa's real GDP growth. During this time, Africa's average growth was 5.6 percent per year (Kaberuka 2010, p. 2-3) which has turned Africa into one of the fastest growing regions in the world and pushed it to reach the same level like Brazil or the Russian Federation (Leke *et al.* 2010). The forecasted real GDP growth of 5.2 percent in 2011 is based on the increasing demand for commodities and the general recovering of the economies after the financial crisis (Kaberuka 2010, p. 2). Regarding Collier (2010a, p. 3) this development is "[...] underwritten by growing Asian economies and their corresponding need for commodities. All of this is in line with the concern of the United States Congress House of Representatives (2008, p. 28) that China is strongly involved in Africa by gaining access to raw materials and Luedi's (2008, pp. 76-80) findings on China's geopolitical strategy to control strategic assets. Luedi assessed all M&A activities of Chinese companies between 1995 and 2007. Since 2003, Chinese FDI in organic growth reached $2.9 billion which increased continually up to $30.1 billion in 2007. Furthermore, 80 percent of Chinese FDI were made by state-owned TNCs. FDI are based on many strategic rationales and are invested in a wide range of diversified industries, but "the first transaction aim was primarily to gain secure access to supplies of critical raw material." In his book 'The Plundered Planet' Collier (2010b, pp. 91-130) categorized China's behaviour and its geopolitical strategy as a new colonialism. In the future, Africa will be definitely one of the primary targets in terms of geopolitical strategies. "Africa is the last region on earth that remains largely unexplored" and if these "untapped resources have been discovered, Africa's commodity exports will be around five times of the current level" (Collier 2010a, p. 3).

2.4 Natural resources management — ways to secure access to raw material based on the European Union's view

Köhler (2011, p. 2)[14] asserts: "Europe needs Africa for its raw material supply and future markets. In the year 2050, Africa will have more than two billion inhabitants — four times more than Europe. The Chinese have already recognized the importance of this continent."[15] However, there is a general challenge regarding commodity prices and raw materials. A McKinsey survey (2010, p. 6) reports that the increasing supply or usage of natural resources has an impact on companies' profit. Especially in the energy and manufacturing sector there are still concerns about possible negative effects. This negative point of view is shared by 45 percent of the executives of the manufacturing sector and 34 percent of the energy sector executives. Dittmann[16],

---

[14] Former IMF Managing Director, former Chairman of the Executive Board of the IMF and former Federal President of Germany from 2004 to 2010. STIFTUNG HAUS DER GESCHICHTE DER BUNDESREPUBLIK DEUTSCHLAND. 2011. *Biografie: Horst Köhler* [online]. [Accessed July 14th, 2011]. Available from: http://www.hdg.de/lemo/html/biografien/KoehlerHorst/index.html.

[15] Original quotation: "Europa braucht Afrika für seine Rohstoffversorgung und künftige Wachstumsmärkte. Im Jahr 2050 wird es mehr als zwei Milliarden Afrikaner geben – viermal so viele wie Europäer. Die Chinesen haben die neue Bedeutung dieses Kontinents längst erkannt."

[16] Managing Director European Affairs, BDI, Federation of German Industries

states: "It is important to address access to raw materials because this is not as easy as it used to be. This is partly due to increased demand. These raw materials are necessary for technological industry and without guidance and support the industry is unable to solve the problem on their own. It needs a strong political environment on the national and European level" (Eurometaux - European Association of Metals 2011). Regarding these observations and concerns the EU Commission launched in 2008 the "Raw Materials Initiative" (RMI) (European Commission 2011e; European Commission 2008) and established an integrated strategy for defining policies for raw materials for responding to the different challenges of high demand (European Commission 2011e). The RMI sets up a list of 49 "potentially critical" raw materials whose availability to industry could come under threat as global competition for natural resources increases (Eurometaux - European Association of Metals 2011) before the EU commissions take actions within this framework to address sustainable access to raw materials both within and outside the EU as well as on resource efficiency and recycling[17]. At the moment, RMI has identified three types of risks (Eurometaux - European Association of Metals 2011):

- Import risk, where raw materials are imported from a politically instable region or from a country where the market economy does not work based on the World Bank's governance indexes which measure the political and economic stability indexes of countries.

- Production risk within the EU, with potential problems such as land access.

- Environmental risk, based on indicators such as air or soil pollution, where the impact of the use of raw materials is measured from an environmental point of view.

These risks can be reduced by natural resources management. On the EU supra-national level the overall strategy to reduce these risks and to find future availability of

---

[17] This work is part of the Europe 2020 strategy to ensure smart, sustainable and inclusive growth and is closely linked to the flagship initiative for a resource efficient Europe EUROPEAN COMMISSION. 2011e. *Tackling the challenges in commodity markets and on raw materials.* Brussels: European Union.

certain materials and resources is (Eurometaux - European Association of Metals 2011):

- Reducing consumption of primary natural resources by increasing resources efficiency and recycling;

- Finding substitutions by other raw materials;

- Trying to find raw materials within Europe;

- Fighting for free and fair markets;

- Establishing strategy relationships.

From a theoretical perspective there are three possibilities to ensure direct access to natural resources (Dye and Stephenson 2010, p. 7):

- Building relationships with governments to ensure access to natural resources;

- Ensuring that natural resources are affordable for hedging;

- Investing directly to procure natural resources.

The last one will be analysed in the publication in the following chapters.

3 Methodology

The existing literature presented in the last chapter illustrates the shift of global economic power and scarcity of natural resources as well as the involvement of the state. Due to this a holistic approach is necessary to understand the different interest groups within the EU and in the developing countries.

This publication extends the present literature by conducting an own survey and proposes a new approach of defence in the war of resources for the EU. It will tie in with the theoretical idea of direct investments to procure natural resources. Therefore, it will explore the possibility and importance of SWFs as an adequate instrument for EU to secure access to critical raw materials. The approach and results are analysed in respect to the legal framework.

3.1 Setting of the descriptive study

The survey is using a descriptive research approach to identify and describe the area of SWFs and their applicability as strategic investment vehicles. The author chose this method as the most appropriate one to receive and compare different opinions on different phenomena. With respect to the EU and international discussions about the scarcity of resources and state geopolitical strategies the research question "Is a strategic SWF investment an adequate instrument in general and for the EU to secure access to critical raw material?" is addressed by using two different questionnaires for different target groups. One questionnaire addressed SWFs directly; the other one addressed economic research experts which are often employed within the large banks in the EU and the US as well asset management firms. This is due to the fact that no clear definition of SWFs exists and due to the limited disclosure and lack of transparency (United Nations 2010a, p. 27). A mail questionnaire has been developed.

It is assumed that both target groups hold different point of views concerning the research question due to the following:

- SWFs have different characteristics as state-owned investment vehicles and therefore follow different missions. These missions reflect different political systems. They have big impacts on economic and political decisions. Regarding Shemirani (2011, p. XII) "[...] decision making processes based solely on either political or economic considerations are often inefficient since they often fail to account for important benefits that an SWF invests. The politically-based decisions discount the potential economic benefit that SWF investments may have on the host economy. For instance, SWFs can provide long-term liquidity when short-term liquidity is tight and markets are contracting." Due to this and based on the fact that SWFs diversify the global investor base they can have a large influence on market efficiency and lower volatility. SWFs could also drive market prices by controlling the physical assets either by holding the assets or buying them. Due to this reason the 46 largest SWFs mentioned by the SWF Institute Fund ranking are identified as potential participants for the survey (SWF Institute 2011). The chosen participants reflect the whole range of SWFs in kind of region, political system, assets under management, degree of transparency and source of investment.

- Economic research experts are responsible for macroeconomic analysis within their companies. They analyse relevant trends for the bank and asset management firms in financial markets, the economy and society and highlight risks and opportunities. Focus research topics are often macroeconomic analysis and analysis of growth trends, economic policy issues in Europe and in the US, global research on the financial sector and its regulation, and natural resources — risks and opportunities, ensuring future supply. Generally, economic researchers act as consultants for banks and large institutional clients. Due to this fact researchers have a huge influence on general investment decisions (Meyer 2011). Private and state institutional investors as well as banks, which have financial intermediation functions, are large financial investors. Between 2003 and 2008 institutional investors increased their investments in commodity markets from €13 billion to €170 billion to €222 billion (European Commission 2011e, p. 2). The theory of financial intermediation is explained in the appendix 5.

Furthermore, banks are involved in the capital markets on their own risk and on their own books. It can be summarized that both functions turn banks into leading actors in the capital markets which also have an influence on market prices. The European

Commission (2011e, p. 6) argues that there is a growing interdependence of commodities and related financial markets. These activities are normally based on the advice of economic research experts. Due to this reason the economic researchers of 45 institutions are part of this survey to develop an idea of the banks' future advice.

The SWF survey is supposed to figure out if SWFs invest in natural resources and the research survey asks if an SWF is a possible solution for the EU. Furthermore, the conformities or differences of the views will be analysed and explored in this publication. Moreover, to improve the quality of the data the questionnaire methods will exanimate of secondary sources (Saunders, Lewis and Thornhill 2009, p. 362).

3.2   Survey research strategy

The overall research strategy of the publication is based on a deductive survey to use and collect quantitative data, which can be analysed quantitatively using descriptive and inferential statistics. Regarding Saunders (Saunders, Lewis and Thornhill 2009, p. 144) the collected data allow to generate findings that represent the opinion of the participants on this research question. This is based on rating questions which are regarded as indicators to answer the research question (Saunders, Lewis and Thornhill 2009, p. 378). Chapter 2.3 already described and observed the possibility of assuring access to natural resources by state-owned enterprises in certain countries.

The data collection for the analysis of the research questions is based on a questionnaire, which comprises the view of SWFs and researchers to figure out if SWFs did invest in critical raw materials and if an SWF is a possible instrument for the EU.

For the quantitative data collection a questionnaire has been used to reach a wide range of participants worldwide. Survey questions were adapted from the review of literature. The set of questions was send via email as a self-administrated pdf-questionnaire to the participants with a clear guideline describing the purpose and the proceedings of the questionnaire.

The collected data of the survey will be evaluated with the help of a descriptive data analysis. The results of the survey will afterwards be completed and supported by secondary sources.

4 Analysis and results of the empirical survey

4.1 Sovereign Wealth Funds survey

The survey is intended to figure out if SWFs invest in natural resources. The sent-out questionnaire led to a zero response rate. This fact has to be analysed and interpreted. The interpretation and the original aim is supported by literature to make a contribution to the publication. The questionnaire's design is attached in the appendices 1 and 2.

4.1.1 Zero response rate of Sovereign Wealth Funds survey

The survey was supposed to be sent to 46 SWFs. 15 SWFs did not provide contact addresses on their websites. Due to that the number was reduced to 31. Three SWFs were contacted via an online portal. Therefore, the request to participate was sent out without an attachment based on the fact that there was no response and no possibility to check the submission, consequently the universal set of the survey had to be reduced. Finally, the questionnaire was sent out to 28 SWFs — four of which provided a personal email address. 24 questionnaires were sent out to general email address like contact@name_of_SWF[...] or investor@name_of_SWF[...]. Two out of the 28 sent-out requests created an error message, so that only 26 SWFs received the questionnaire. Finally, two SWFs gave the response that they generally do not participate in surveys. Despite a second request addressed to 24 SWFs the response rate was zero.

4.1.2 Aim and interpretation of the survey

The aim of the survey was to figure out and support the literature regarding the question if SWFs strongly invest in natural resources especially in minerals and metals or not and due to this fact to develop a possible solution for the access to scarce resources. Based on the fact that official information about SWFs' investment is not available and comprehensive, the SWFs were questioned about the following topics that can be labelled to three categories:

- Investment strategy and development (questions 1 to 3)
- General questions about the development of natural resources (questions 4 to 6)

- Specific questions about SWF investment in natural resources split by sources and regions (questions 7 to 9)

Regarding the survey's response rate also with respect to the fact that the Australian and the Norwegian SWFs responded that they generally do not participate in surveys it becomes obviously that "the GAAP is a voluntary set of principles and practices" (Suwaidi and Caruana 2008) which is not generally accepted or maybe still not really implemented. With the help of the literature two results can be interpreted for the survey:

1. Many SWFs belong to countries with a socialist economic system (Avendaño and Santiso 2010) which particularly don't invest in natural resources through SWFs but through state-owned enterprises (Research expert's survey).

2. SWFs generally invest in natural resources but also in minerals and metals. In H1 2010 around 9 percent of their investment volume has flown into the mining sector and around 10 percent into the coal, petroleum and natural gas industry. This also reflects their activities in terms of numbers for target investment (7 percent and 10 percent) (Bolton and Samama 2010, p. 9).

This led to the conclusion that SWFs invest in natural resources as well as minerals and metals either because of financial motives based on increasing commodity prices or political motives based on the strategic relevance of these elements.

4.2 Research experts' survey

The survey was supported by well-known economic research experts of the financial markets industry and research institutions of Sovereign Wealth Funds. The questionnaire's design and the results are attached in the appendices 2 to 3.

4.2.1 Research experts' survey with accurate measurements return rate

The survey has been sent out to 45 researchers from financial institutions. 12 of these were contacted via an online portal. Therefore, the request to participate was sent out without an attachment based on the fact that there was no response and no possibility to check the submission the universal set of the survey had to be reduced. Also these 12 were not contacted for the second request. Finally, the questionnaire was sent out to 33 research experts. From the 33 sent-out surveys 14 respondents answered and 11 have successfully completed and returned the survey. Two out of the 11 returned questionnaires were returned after the second request. This led to a response rate of 33,33 percent. In general, a survey should have a high response rate to work on a 95 percent level of certainty to represent the characteristics of the population or industry (Saunders, Lewis and Thornhill 2009, pp. 218-219). Regarding Visser, Krosnick, Marquette, & Curtin (1996) the survey results with a response rate of 33,33 percent yielded more accurate measurements than those with a higher response rate of nearly 60 or 70 percent based on the multifaceted topic of the publication in general and the survey in particular.

4.2.2 Results and analysis of the survey

Analysing the questionnaire the result of the eight different questions is illustrated in an eight bar diagram. The type of question is summarized in the headline of each figure. The y-axis of the bar diagram shows the rating scale and illustrates how strong the respondents agree or disagree with a different statement which are formulated as closed questions. The scale is defined in Table 3.

Table 3: Scale of statement value

1	Strongly agree
2	Agree
3	Disagree
4	Strongly disagree
0	Not evaluated

The x-axis describes the eleven respondents. The last dark blue bar illustrates the mean[18]. The numbers in the right corner of the diagram show the standard deviation which measures the spread from the mean[19].

---

[18] Mean defines the value of each question divided by the total number of respondents.
[19] Standard deviation describes the spread from the mean.

Question 1: 'The EU's future economic growth is threatened by a scarcity of natural resources especially in terms of minerals and metals.'

The findings that are illustrated in

Figure 15 show that the EU's future growth is not depending on or threatened by the scarcity of natural resources in particular. The mean of all answers is close to 'disagree.' Regarding the comment of the questionnaire "In as far as the world's resources are limited, this statement is true for any economy, incl. the EU. Problem: The EU has a strong industrial base which could actually benefit directly from immediate access to raw materials but is not threatened only by this factor" (Questionnaire 1).

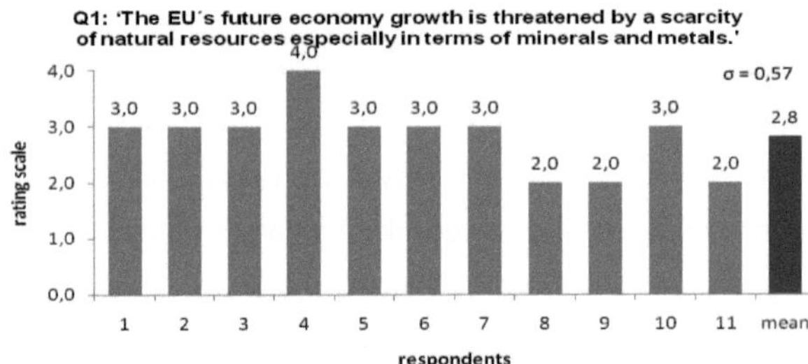

Figure 15: Results of question 1

<u>Question 2:</u> 'Governments should take an important and active role to secure access to critical resources.'

The results of question 2 (see Figure 16) with a mean of 2.4 indicate that capital market participants see a need for governmental involvement. The standard deviation is 0.88 which means that there is a high range of different options but six out of eleven agree or strongly agree to the question.

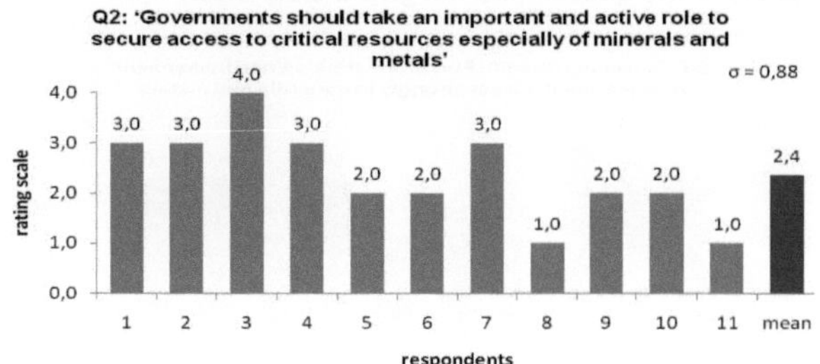

Figure 16: Results of question 2

<u>Question 3:</u> 'Developing and transition economies take advantage through governmental investments in minerals and metals.'

The result of question 3 (see Figure 17) shows that over 80 percent of the respondents see competitive distortions, which are underlined with a mean of 2.0.

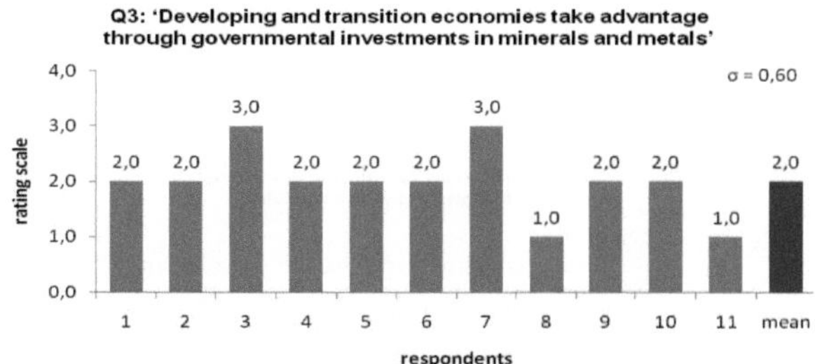

Figure 17: Results of question 3

Question 4: 'Sovereign Wealth Funds are state-owned investment vehicles which invest strongly in minerals and metals.'

The results (see Figure 18) show that over 45 percent see SWFs as an instrument which governments use in the war of resources. Nearly 55 percent do not see SWFs in general as state-owned vehicles which invest strongly in minerals and metals. One respondent who disagreed, comments "only a limited number do" (see questionnaire 1, p. 3). The results of the question do not give a clear view.

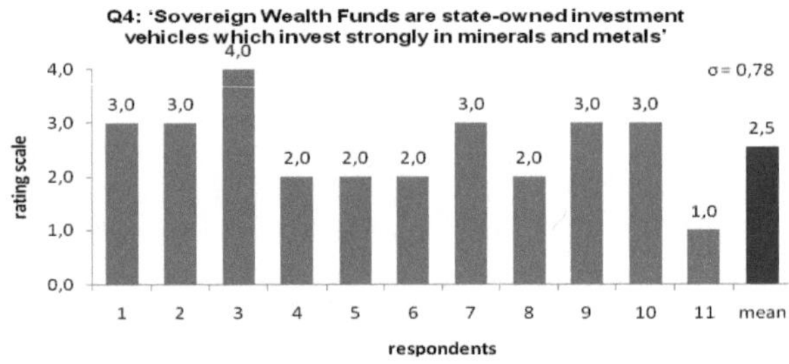

Figure 18: Results of question 4

Question 5: 'The European Union (EU) is a conglomerate of national states who speak and act with one voice.'

The respondents clearly 'disagree' to this question. The mean of 3.0 and a standard deviation of 0.30 underline this inference (see Figure 19). The respondent displayed on number one comments 'depending on the issue.' Therefore, the box was not checked (questionnaire 1, p. 3).

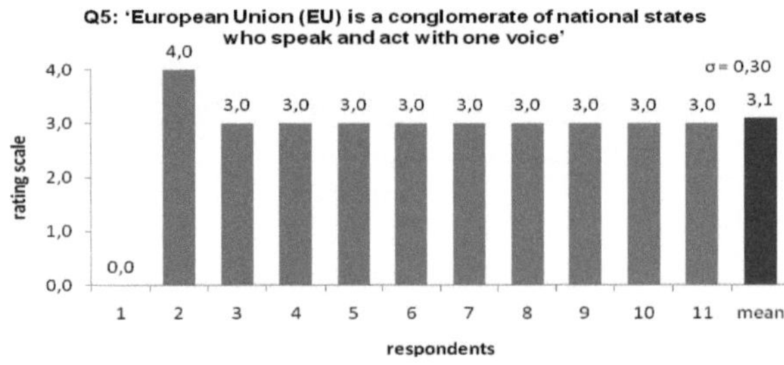

Figure 19: Results of question 5

Question 6: 'The European Union (EU) is able to operate conjointly in financial and economic affairs.'

In general, the respondents say that the EU works better concerning financial issues rather than concerning general affairs (see Figure 20). All respondents voted equal or better than on questions 5. Only the respondent who appears as number 11 disagrees. This led to the fact that the mean did not tend to move closer to 2 compared to the mean of question 5 with 3,1. One respondent commented: "less than they might or should" (see questionnaire).

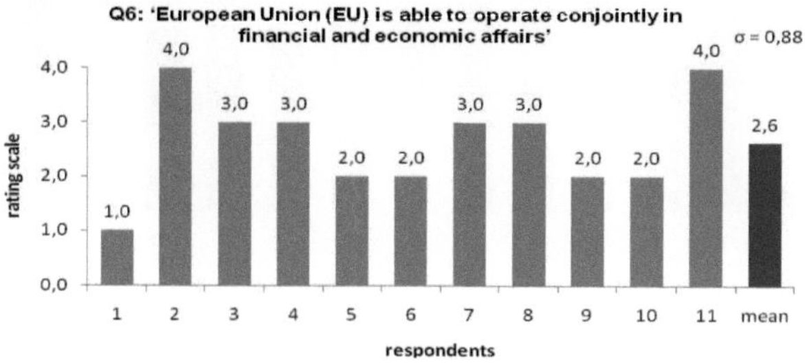

Figure 20: Results of question 6

Question 7: 'The European Union (EU) should increase its activities to invest directly to procure natural resources.'

The mean is 2.8 and 72 percent of the respondents disagreed or strongly disagreed to the question (see Figure 21).

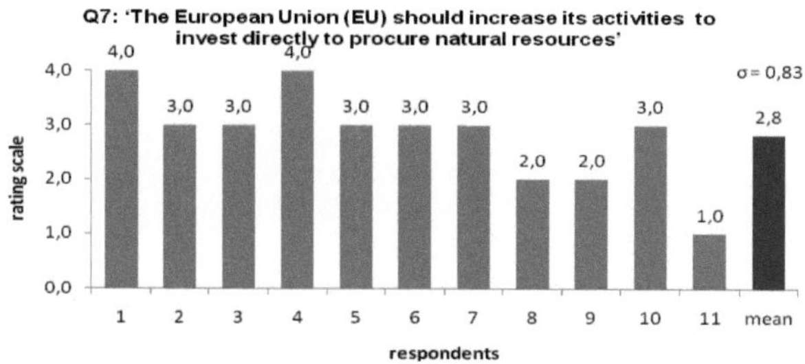

Figure 21: Results of question 7

<u>Question 8:</u> 'A "European Union SWF" could be an adequate instrument to ensure direct access to natural resources.'

The results of the last question (see Figure 22) point out that capital market experts from the western world are strictly against a "European Union SWF." 100 percent of the respondents don't see strategic SWF investments as a possible solution in the war of resources for the European Union.

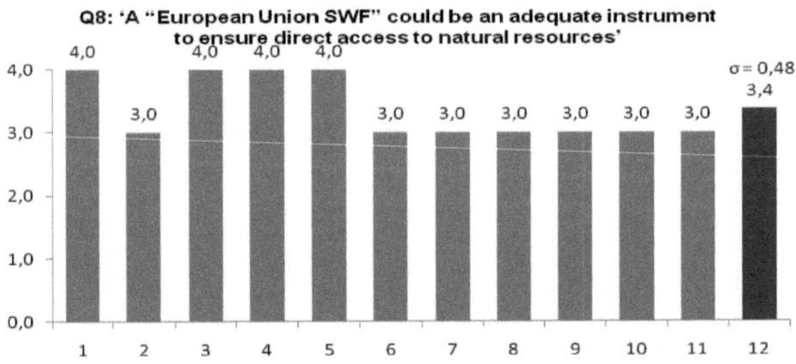

Figure 22: Results of question 8

4.2.3 Summary

The statements of the questionnaire and the results will be interpreted. Figure 23 provides an overview of the questions related to the research question.

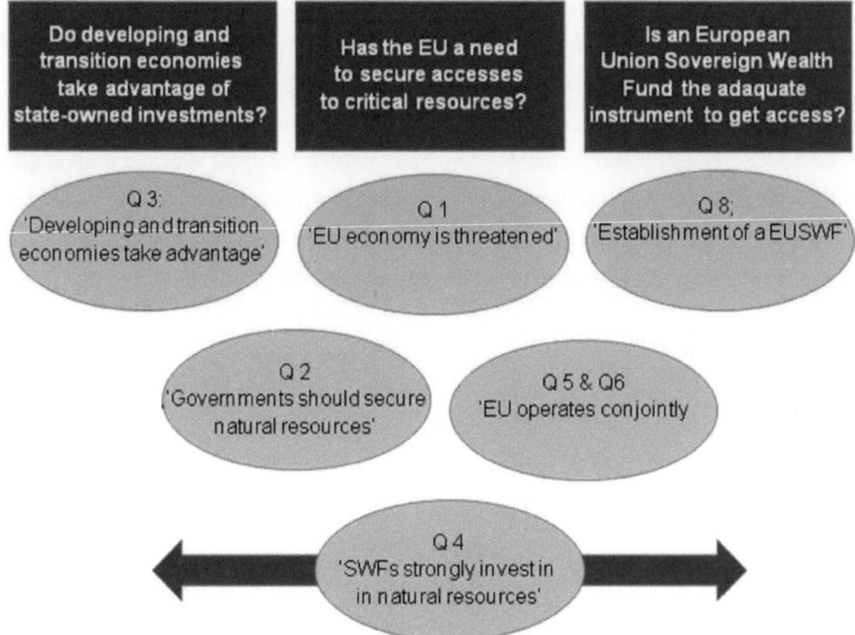

Figure 23: Relationship between research question and questionnaire

The results of the survey show that the EU is disable to work conjointly as one nation. On the one hand side, the experts do not see a direct threat of EU growth in the context of scarcity of natural resources. On the other hand side, the experts agree to the statement that the developing and transition economies participate based on governmental investments. Both factors support the denial of a EUSWF. However, based on the missing results from the SWFs it is not clear if an SWF an appropriate instrument to invest in natural resources. This is in line with two facts. Not all SWFs invest in minerals (especially the Generation Funds) and "SWFs are only one opportunity to get strategic access to real assets." For example, "China tries to get access to state-owned enterprises through buying direct participants or take over commodity-based enterprises" (questionnaire 10). Particularly, they require that governments should secure access to natural resources. To summarize the results: Developing and transition economies have an advantage to directly invest in natural resources. In terms of the EU a EUSWF is not a solution because on the one hand side they miss the will to work together and on the other hand side state-owned investments are against the ideology of the EU economy or possible for financial founding. The following comment from the questionnaire supports this view: "The EU and the member states lack the financial resources to join that game [...]. Focus should be on promoting high value-added industries and on establishing good political relations with key trading and production partners around the world." "Good political relations with resource-rich and manufacturing economies (China, Russian Federation, Brazil) are nowadays more important than direct access to resources" (questionnaire 1).

5   Discussion, implications and limitations of the findings

The research assesses that the natural resources are limited. The world economy is threatened by a scarcity therefore the EU's future is not threatened in any special way by a scarcity of natural resources because also any other economy is facing this situation. This is supported by the survey's comment: "In as far as the world's resources are limited, the EU's future economy is threatened by a scarcity of natural resources especially in terms of minerals and metals but also for any other economy on the world" (questionnaire 1). The results of the survey have to be discussed in the context of the current literature to answer the research questions and to make improvements to the current EU behaviour in the war of resources. Furthermore, limitations of the research and future enhancement in this field of research will be mentioned.

5.1   The benefit of Sovereign Wealth Funds as a question of the economic system

The research found out that the EU does not have an SWF and that the financial actors also do not want an EUSWF in the future. Despite, the survey shows that many Asian and oil producing countries have SWFs or state-owned enterprises and therefore an advantage in the war of the resources. In order to explain this, the different economic ideologies and systems are analysed. Indeed the analysis will not include the discussions concerning the independence between economic and political systems.

5.1.1 Capitalist system versus socialist system

As a matter of fact, there are two worldwide ideologies featuring their own political and economic systems. The capitalist system and the socialist system, which is often called "communist system" (Kornai 2000, p. 27). In the Eastern Asian economies we prominently observe socialist systems. Meaning they believe in market-based state-aided economic growth (Dahrendorf 1990, p. 8). In this region some of the world's most populated countries like China are located. The countries in the EU and the US have chosen the capitalist system[20]. Figure 24 provides a useful way of illustrating the two different systems. The model focuses on the basic specific characteristics in order to discern the two systems.

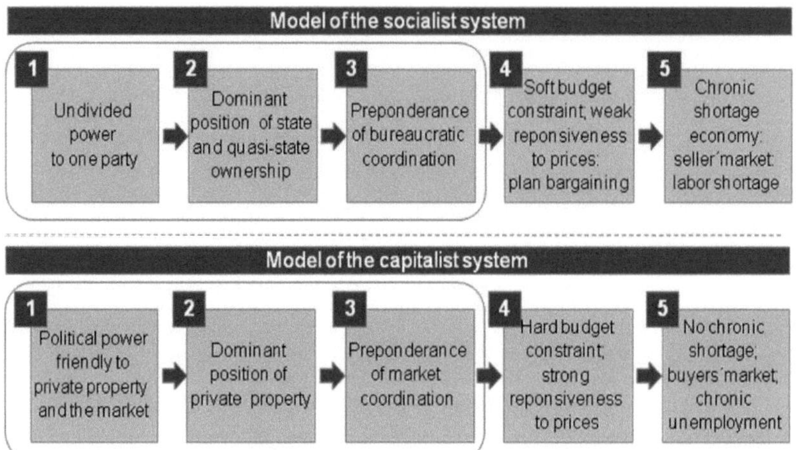

Figure 24: Model of the socialist and capitalist systems (Komai 2000, p. 29)

From block one to three the model shows different attributes influencing different phenomena in terms of typical behaviour of the actors and typical implications of the system. Block one indicates the difference in power distribution from one party to more parties. Furthermore, for the capitalist system a stronger will of friendly opinion in terms of private property and the free market means free enterprises and freedom of contracts, which is missing in the socialist system. The second block stresses the distribution between state-owned property and private-owned property. The third block mentions that the capitalist system prefers a dominance of market coordination. But also that its parties accept the influence and existence of other coordination mechanisms like bureaucratic intervention e.g. cartel authority and that the socialist system prefers statewise and bureaucratic coordination.

In reality it is not possible to draw a clear line in between the two systems. Both systems include market mechanisms and government intervention for goods, prices and

---

[20] At this point, the working hypothesis is that democratic political systems are based on capitalism — not necessarily vice versa.

labour. Because Smith's (Smith 1976, p. 477) idea of the invisible hand that conjunction is steered by the forces of self-interest, competition as well as supply and demand are just as less affected like planned economies where the consumption is planned and steered by a central player who allocates the demand and supply. For example, China also has private-owned businesses. Germany has a large state-owned banking system with its saving bank (Sparkassen und Landesbanken), France's and Sweden's economies are strongly influenced by bureaucratic intervention (Kornai 2000, p. 30; European Central Bank 2009). Today's capitalist system follows Kornai's (2000, p. 16) comment that "for capitalism to consolidate and operate efficiently, it is essential to have a legal infrastructure that protects private property and enforces private contracts and financial discipline." Furthermore, he mentions the positive influences on economic growth if the government is an active actor.

5.1.2 Strategic European Union Sovereign Wealth Funds — a proper solution or a silly idea?

Chapter 1.1 explains the two different economic systems and regarding to the Bertelsmann Transformation Index (BTI) (Bertelsmann Foundation 2011), which evaluates the development and transformation process in 128 countries, many economies have made the transition from a socialist system to a capitalist system with a market economy based on democracy, but the ideal of a productive, market-based democratic state is still far from becoming the global standard. The literature review underlines these findings and outlines that economies like China, the Russian Federation and the Gulf states implement more aspects of a socialist system than a capitalist system and that these economies have state-owned enterprises and SWFs. With regard to the findings of the survey developing and transition economies like mentioned above benefit from governmental investments in minerals and metals. Consequently, also with respect to the interpretation of the SWF survey (see chapter 4.1) there is no doubt that this — to a certain extent — can be attributed to SWF involvement.

On the other hand side, it is beyond dispute that the single states and also the EU as the conglomerate of these economies have a capitalist system with all its essential features like market economy power and less governmental coordination (see chapter 1.1). The findings in chapter 4 proved that a strategic SWF is not an adequate instrument to ensure direct access to natural resources for the EU. In the context of the literature it is obvious that the idea of a strategic EUSWF is unrealistic for western traditional capitalist economic research as well for these governments.

In general, it can be summarized that an SWF could be an adequate instrument in the war of resources — depending of the economic system. In the case of the EU it is clearly not a solution.

By taking the outlined literature in chapter 2.2 into consideration two facts become relevant:

- SWFs were originally established for economic purposes and not for political reasons (Stabilization/Generation Funds). In terms of Exchange SWFs the purpose is to stabilize the exchange rate of the currency.

- SWFs are funded by surplus of or exchange reserves.

As opposed to the two points above it becomes apparent that money must be provided in order to establish an SWF. In the case of the EU this is not an option because of the large indebtedness (see chapter 2.1 and Figure 8). Finally, the survey mentions the problem of a commitment to operate conjointly in financial and economic affairs in the EU, which is necessary for funding an SWF. However, the literature shows in the chapter 1.2 and in the survey that there is an important need to get access to raw materials without the approach of direct investments but more in terms of strong political relationships (see chapter 2.4).

5.2 Is the European Union able to embrace future challenges?

The research concluded that the focus should be on establishing good relationships with key trading and production partners worldwide based on a good political relationship with resources-rich and manufacturing economies, organising a stable investment environment, supporting research and development for finding substitutions and for effective technologies. The findings of the survey state that the EU is not able to operate conjointly in financial and economic affairs — this is inconsistent with the literature review that has shown that the EU already launched the RMI. In addition, the survey emphasizes that the EU in general is a conglomerate of national states which is not able to speak and act with one voice. This inconsistency has to be analysed and discussed.

5.2.1 Framework for the evaluation of the Raw Material Initiative behaviour

The evaluation of the RMI as part of the EU behaviour will be conducted by using Chaffey's (2009, pp. 265-267) 'Generic strategy process model.' This model combines all essential aspects of a strategy and explicitly refers to the fact that there exists an organic view on strategy formulation and implementation, which enables to going backwards and forwards between the single strategy elements. This approach ensures a better adaptability and responsiveness to changing internal and external environmental factors and is based on the work of Mintzberg and Quinn from 1995 and Lynch from 2000 (Chaffey 2009, p. 267). Both academics distinguish between a prescriptive[21] and an emergent[22] strategy approach (Chaffey 2009, p. 267). Figure 25 illustrates the combined model of Chaffey with the five important steps to successfully implement a strategy.

---

[21] Prescriptive strategy: The three core areas of strategic analysis, development and strategy implementation are linked together sequentially.

[22] Emergent strategy: Strategic analysis, strategic development and strategy implementation are interrelated.

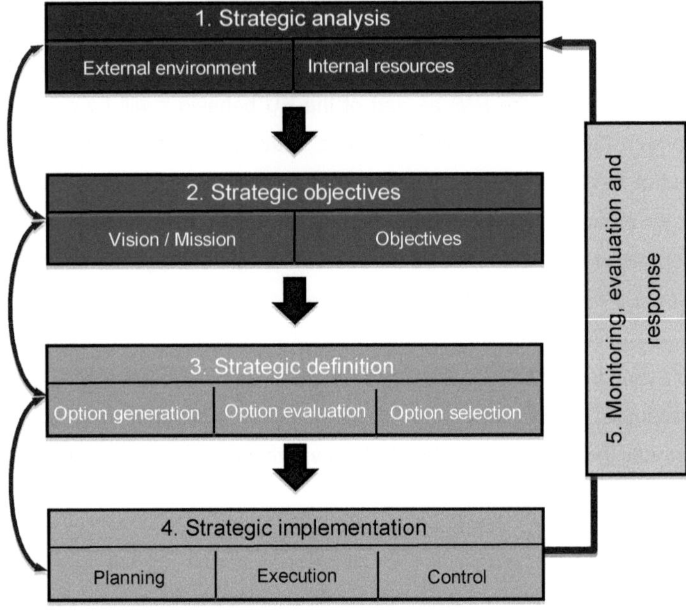

Figure 25: Generic Strategy Process Model (Chaffey 2009, p. 267)

The model allows to check the direction and scope of initiative over the long term and if it achieves an advantage for the EU through its configuration of resources within a changing environment to meet the challenges and to fulfil the stakeholder's (national government) expectations (Johnson, Scholes and Whittington 2008, p. 3).

5.2.1 Evaluation of the European Union Raw Material Initiative behaviour

Since the RMI has been launched in 2008 the European Commission of Trade has on two occasions communicated the work of the RMI to the decision-making body of the EU, the European Parliament and the Council. The first time was in 2008 after the launch and the second time in February 2011 to report on the progress made during the implementation (European Commission 2011d). The effectiveness of the RMI will be evaluated related to Chaffey's strategy model consisting of five steps. Figure 26 gives an overview of EU RMI strategy and the evaluation of the results.

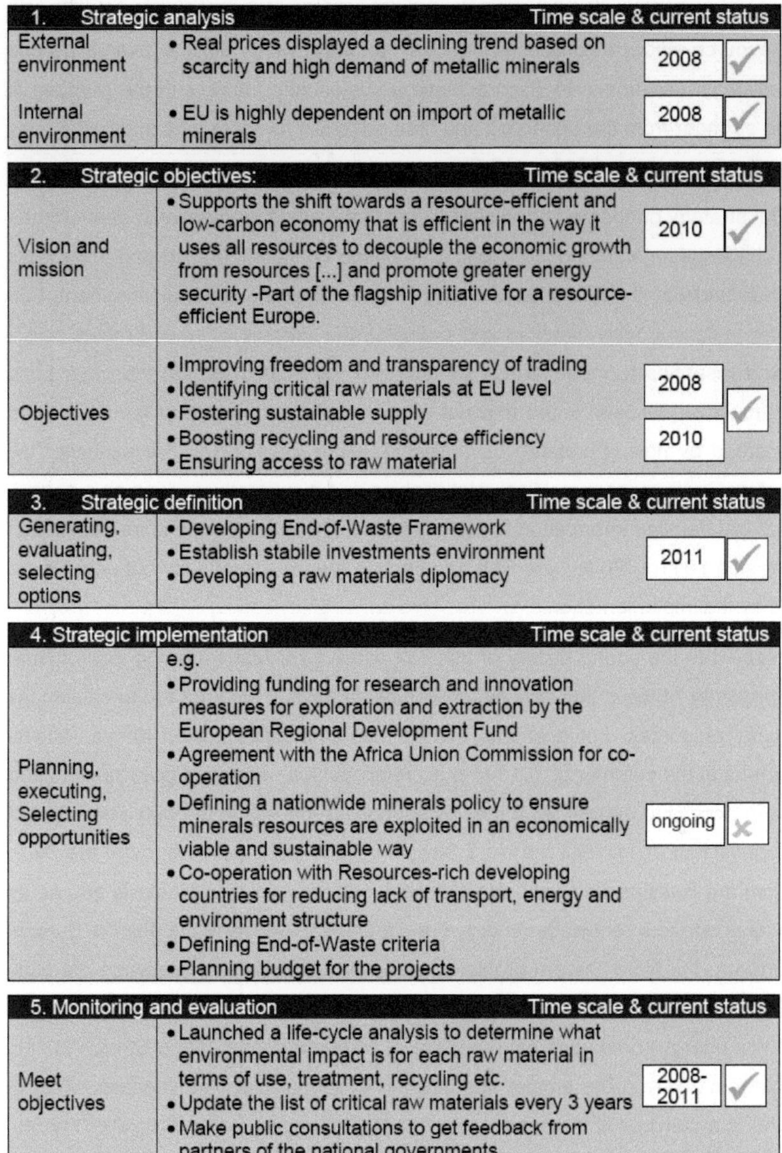

1. Strategic analysis		Time scale & current status
External environment	• Real prices displayed a declining trend based on scarcity and high demand of metallic minerals	2008 ✓
Internal environment	• EU is highly dependent on import of metallic minerals	2008 ✓

2. Strategic objectives:		Time scale & current status
Vision and mission	• Supports the shift towards a resource-efficient and low-carbon economy that is efficient in the way it uses all resources to decouple the economic growth from resources [...] and promote greater energy security -Part of the flagship initiative for a resource-efficient Europe.	2010 ✓
Objectives	• Improving freedom and transparency of trading • Identifying critical raw materials at EU level • Fostering sustainable supply • Boosting recycling and resource efficiency • Ensuring access to raw material	2008 2010 ✓

3. Strategic definition		Time scale & current status
Generating, evaluating, selecting options	• Developing End-of-Waste Framework • Establish stabile investments environment • Developing a raw materials diplomacy	2011 ✓

4. Strategic implementation		Time scale & current status
Planning, executing, Selecting opportunities	e.g. • Providing funding for research and innovation measures for exploration and extraction by the European Regional Development Fund • Agreement with the Africa Union Commission for co-operation • Defining a nationwide minerals policy to ensure minerals resources are exploited in an economically viable and sustainable way • Co-operation with Resources-rich developing countries for reducing lack of transport, energy and environment structure • Defining End-of-Waste criteria • Planning budget for the projects	ongoing ✗

5. Monitoring and evaluation		Time scale & current status
Meet objectives	• Launched a life-cycle analysis to determine what environmental impact is for each raw material in terms of use, treatment, recycling etc. • Update the list of critical raw materials every 3 years • Make public consultations to get feedback from partners of the national governments	2008-2011 ✓

Figure 26: Evaluation of the EU RMI strategy

(*Author's own based on* European Commission 2008, 2011d)

With reference to Figure 26 it can be said that the RMI as part of the flagship initiative for a resource-efficient Europe has a clear strategy, which fits the overall Europe 2020 strategy (see appendix 6) to achieve a sustainable future with the purpose to emerge stronger from the economic and financial crisis for more jobs and better lives (European Commission 2010, pp. 2-7).

The RMI strategy on the one hand side shows that it has the potential to deal with the future challenges mentioned in chapter 2 — based on clearly framed and achievable objectives and well-thought options after a stringent analysis of the environment. Furthermore, it continuously monitors and evaluates the strategy whether it meets objectives and responds to meanderings by adapting the objectives. On the other hand side, it must be critically noted that not all of the planned opportunities have been implemented by now (European Commission 2011e, pp. 12-17). For example, the RMI has not built up many political relationships and is currently working on a consultation to get detailed information to identify future innovation partnerships (European Commission 2011c). So far, the RMI approaches are on a good way but seem to be trigged by the implementation.

With respect to the young history of the RMI and a particularly missing implementation it becomes obvious that national governments have to work on future challenges for natural resources. For example, the German Chancellor visited Kenya, Angola and Nigeria in the summer of 2011 to build relationships with these governments and to ensure access to natural resources by supporting the region through development aid (Tagesschau 2011). But the Nord Stream natural gas pipeline through the Baltic Sea from the Russian Federation to Germany secures access to natural gas as an essential bridge to a renewable energy era not only for Germany but also for Europe. Furthermore, the Nord Stream project is primarily a co-operation between the Russian gas export monopolist Gazprom and German energy companies but also French and Dutch energy companies have a stake of 15 percent each (Nord Stream 2011b; Nord Stream 2011a). The project was initiated by former German Chancellor Schröder, who is a member of the supervisory board. The example also illustrates that solutions on a national level are not a viable option. Summarizing the evaluation of RMI compared to the activities on the national level leads to the conclusion that the right strategy to fight the war of resources could only be set up on a supra-national level.

Getting back to the question if the EU is able to conjointly act on future challenges the following can be outlined. The survey is right that the EU currently works conjointly less than they might or should and that there is more potential. But considering the European 2020 strategy paper (European Commission 2010, pp. 1-37) it is also right that Europe momentarily faces a phase of transformation. This process has started in 2010 after the financial crisis and currently Europe already acts collectively, as a Union, to overcome the debt crisis. Europe can achieve its vision to get through the crisis and turn the EU into a smart, sustainable and inclusive economy with high levels of employment, productivity and social cohesion. Nevertheless, as long as the EU is not endorsed as a political institution it only builds the framework and sets the conditions. The success depends on national governments and institutions. For this reason and to ensure that each member state adapts the Europe 2020 strategy to its particular situation, the Commission proposes that the EU goals are translated into national targets and trajectories. At this point, the mentioned Europe 2020 circumstance is also appropriate for the RMI, which allows to interpret the survey's results.

5.3 Limitations of the research and future enhancement

The publication explored many findings with regard to the research question and objectives. There are still several aspects where further research would be necessary in the field of natural resources, opportunities for SWFs and activities of the EU in the war of resources.

In the following, the cognition gained from this publication is listed and suggestions for improvements will be made.

General research

- Without a doubt, SWFs are a complex area of research. Chapter 2.2.3 mentioned that SWFs are not transparent. The original research was intended to first figure out if SWFs in general can be a solution in the war of natural resources. Due to this the primary research (survey) was supposed to figure out if SWFs invest in minerals and metals also to get a deeper insight of the whereabouts and the amounts invested. Based on the survey results the advantages and disadvantages have been analysed to discuss the question in general if an SWF is a possible solution in the war of resources. Thereafter, based on these results, the possibility of an EUSWF has been discussed at the end of the publication. The limited literature and the zero response to this topic led to an adjustment of the research. Consequently, an expert survey has been developed during the writing process with a stronger focus on the EU activities in general.

Improvements

A different approach may have led to a different research question because it has been known that SWFs are not transparent and for that reason dealing with this topic can be risky. This fact was also mentioned in the proposal. Nevertheless, the problem to figure out if SWFs invest and where and how much has come up during the writing of the literature review and the methodology to prepare the survey. Therefore, it would have been more appropriate to focus on the EU measurements like the RMI rather than only on SWFs as a possible solution. Definitely, this is the lesson learned during this process.

Survey

- As mentioned above, problems with the general research on this topic had to be dealt with. However, the fact that the SWF survey led to a zero response rate has to be critically scrutinised.

Improvements

Perhaps the questions could have been formulated less complex. As for example, single questions instead of complex matrices (see questionnaire). Nevertheless, comparable studies about SWFs had to deal with the same problems. This fact is also reflected in the answers of the only two SWFs that have responded, stating that they generally do not participate in surveys. Finally, the author was aware of this challenge which has been mentioned in the proposal. Furthermore, the publication explains the reasons for this challenge by emphasizing that SWFs more or less face a lack of transparency.

- The results of the economic research experts' survey particularly differ from the results of other studies and the literature.

Improvements

A different phrasing or a different order of the questions could have led to different results. For example, question 1 'The EU's future economic growth is threatened by a scarcity of natural resources especially in terms of minerals and metals' could have been split into five single questions:

- 'Is there a scarcity of natural resources?'

- 'Is there a scarcity of minerals and metals?'

- 'Do natural resources have a strategic importance for EU industries?'

- 'Do certain minerals and metals have a strategic importance for EU industries?'

- 'Is there a necessity for the EU to take action in terms of natural resources?'

Indeed, the author has proved the question with the help of an expert. Furthermore, the author decided to use the least possible amount of questions for the survey to increase the likelihood of a high response rate. The accomplished survey achieved a response rate of 33 percent.

Future enhancement

- The findings of the survey clearly and consistently explain that an SWF is not a possible solution for the EU in the war of resources to ensure direct access to natural resources. These findings are based on the survey's results by asking research experts from the financial industry and respectively from different economic systems.

Improvements

Taking a completely different approach and recommend the establishment of an SWF in the EU as a defending strategy also in the war of resources may have led to different results. This is based on the fact that national governments already have laws of defending[23]. Generally speaking these certain laws provide governments with the right to prevent FDI in their countries (Deutsche Steuerrecht 2008; United States General Accounting Office 1996). This is not in line with EU law. Article 56 says: "[...] all restrictions on the movement of capital between Member States and between Member States and third countries shall be prohibited." Article 58 permits measures which are justified on grounds of public policies or public security — but in reality it can be observed that these are not clearly enough defined (European Commission 2011f). In this context an EUSWF could be evaluated as an 'If you can't beat them, join them' approach. In this case politicians rather than economic researchers have to be involved. Furthermore, the legal framework for the setting up of an EUSWF should be analysed.

- The general research topic moved within the disciplines of applied economics, international policy affairs, legal and regulation terms as well as international business. Therefore, it has been a great challenge to get a hold of available and consistent information and data.

Improvements

For exploring and discovering this research topic in all its fascinating and complex facets, and to provide future enhancement a research centre like the CIBUL is necessarily optimally endowed with excellent knowledge, long-term research opportunities and better social networking and co-operation with other research institutes.

The survey concluded that developing and transition economies such as China take advantages through its state capitalism based on large exchange reverses and a communist system, which also allows them to establish SWFs. And the fact that developed countries like the EU countries do not have capital stocks to establish an SWF — as seen during the current debt crisis — led to the discussion which of the systems plays a predominant role. In 1990, Dahrendorf (1990, p. 8) already stated

---

[23] Examples are the Industry Act of 1975 and the Fair Trading Act of 1973 in the UK, the Foreign Investment Law (1996) in France and the AWG-Novelle in Germany.

that "[…] contemporary capitalist economies seem to thrive on credit rather than savings, on anticipated rather than deferred gratification." The results are reflected in the current debt crisis and a high unemployment rate of 9.4 percent — the group of young people reaching a rate of 20.5 percent[24] (Eurostat 2011, pp. 1-4; Spiegel 2011). This will lead to an expected limited future growth. With reference to Sennett, Professor at the London School of Economics (Twickel 2011, pp. 1-2), all these factors are the reason for the current civil commotions in the UK based on the reduction of social security benefits (especially for employed people) in addition to the large indebtedness and the lack of future perspectives. The behaviour of the neoliberal government in the UK reflects Smith's theory of the invisible hand. At this point, relationships between political and economic systems would have to be analysed as well as evaluated by the different systems. Dahrendorf (1990, p. 7) mentioned that democracy "[...] can be threatened by what one might call, the economic impotence of democracy [...]."

---

[24] The average unemployment rate of the 27 EU countries for young people between 15 — 24 years.

6 Summary

The publication ascertained that there is a scarcity based on natural limitation and increasing prices. Both are driven by a global shift from western economies to eastern economies and a high demand based on increasing population growth and increasing consumption in these regions. Furthermore, the EU strongly depends on imports of important minerals and metals based on the limited natural resources in Europe. Developing and transition economies such as China take advantages of their state capitalism based on increasing GDP growth which leads to increasing exchange reserves. SWFs are only one form of appearance of state capitalism which is working under non-transparency conditions. The EU recognises the threat of scarcity of natural resources and has a need to secure access to critical natural resources. Wherefore it launched the RMI in 2008. After all, the financial markets do not see an EUSWF as a possible solution in the war of resources. This publication outlined different reasons why SWFs in general could be a solution in the war of resources depending on the point of view and ideology. Nevertheless, the limitations of the research require further studies to form an even more grounded opinion.

7 References

AVENDAÑO, R. and J. SANTISO. 2010. Are Sovereign Wealth Fund Investments Politically Biased? Comparing Mutual and Sovereign Funds. *In: Committee on Global Though — "Sovereign Wealth Funds and Other Long-Term Investors "* Columbia University, New York, NY. OECD Development Centre.

BANK OF RUSSIA. 2011. *International Reserves of the Russian Federation from December 2001 to October 2011* [online]. [Accessed August 14th, 2011]. Available from: http://www.cbr.ru/eng/hd_base/mrrf/main_7d.asp?C_mes=12&C_year=2001&To_mes=10&To_year=2011&x=54&y=10&mode=.

BECK, R. and M. FIDORA. 2008. The impact of sovereign wealth funds on global financial markets. *European Central Bank — Occasional Paper Series,* **No 91**(July).

BERRY, G. and X. Y. CHEN. 2001. The Commodity Refiner — Brave New World. *Barclays Capital — Commodities Research* **Spring**.

BERTELSMANN FOUNDATION. 2011. *Transformation Index BTI* [online]. [Accessed August 11th, 2011]. Available from: http://www.bertelsmann-stiftung.de/cps/rde/xchg/SID-6DDA44FA-81068965/bst_engl/hs.xsl/307.htm.

BLESSING, D. 2007. BRICs are chaning the World. *In:* G. SACHS, ed. *HfB-Conference — A brigde to BRIC, Frankfurt School of Finance and Management, Frankfurt.* Goldman Sachs.

BOLTON, P. and F. SAMAMA. 2010. Sovereign Wealth Funds: From Threat To Opportunity. *In: Committee on Global Though — "Sovereign Wealth Funds and other long-term investors", Columbia University, New York, NY.* The Rockefeller Foundation

BOZON, I. J. H., W. J. CAMPBELL and M. LINDSTRAND. 2007. Global trends in energy. *McKinsey Quartlery,* (Number 1).

BREMMER, I. 2009a. State capitalism and the crisis. *McKinsey Quartlery,* (July).

BREMMER, I. 2009b. *State Capitalism Comes of Age* [online]. [Accessed July 24th, 2011]. Available from: http://www.scribd.com/doc/26152824/State-Capitalism-Comes-of-Age-the-End-of-the-Free-Market#archive.

BRESSAND, F., D. FARRELL, P. HAAS, F. MORIN, J. REMES, S. ROEMER, M. ROGERS, J. ROSENFELD and J. WOETZEL. 2007. *Curbing Global Energy Demand Growth: The Energy Productivity Opportunity* McKinsey Global Institute.

BRIDGE, G. 2009. Natural Resources. *In:* K. ROB and T. NIGEL, eds. *International Encyclopedia of Human Geography.* Oxford: Elsevier, p.261 — 268.

BYRAN, L. 2010. Globalization's critical imbalance. *McKinsey Quarterly*, (June).

CENTRAL INTELLIGENCE AGENCY (CIA). 2011. *The World Factbook — Country Comparison: Reserves of foreign exchange and gold* [online]. [Accessed July 14th, 2011]. Available from: https://www.cia.gov/library/publications/the-world-factbook/rankorder/2188rank.html.

CHAFFEY, D. ed. 2009. *E-Business and E-Commerce Management.* Harlow: Prentice Hall.

CLARK, G. L. and A. H. B. MONK. 2010. Sovereign wealth funds: form and function in the 21st century. *In: Committee on Global Though — "Sovereign Wealth Funds and other long-term investors", Columbia University, New York, NY.* Centre for Employment, Work and Finance, Oxford University Centre for the Environment.

COLLIER, P. 2010a. The case for investing in Africa. *McKinsey Quartlery,* (June).

COLLIER, P. 2010b. *The Plundered Planet — Why We Must — And How We Can — Manage Nature for Global Prosperity.* Oxford University Press.

DAHRENDORF, R. 1990. Transitions — Politics, economics and liberty. *Scandinavian Journal of Management,* **6**(1), p3 — 12.

DAVID FOLKERTS-LANDAU. 2011. A User Guide To Commodities. *Deutsche Bank — Global Markets Research.*

DEUTSCHE STEUERRECHT. 2008. *Gesetzgebung: Änderung des AWG und der Außenwirtschaftsverordnung beschlossen* [online]. [Accessed August 12th, 2011].

DYE, R. and E. STEPHENSON. 2010. *Five forces reshaping the global economy.* McKinsey Global Survey results, McKinsey.

EUROMETAUX - EUROPEAN ASSOCIATION OF METALS. 2011. *How Europe can Secure a Fair & Sustainable Supply of Raw Materials from Global Markets* [online]. [Accessed July 7th, 2011]. Available from: http://www.eurometaux.eu/PublicNews/tabid/84/articleType/ArticleView/articleId/166/How-Europe-can-Secure-a-Fair-Sustainable-Supply-of-Raw-Materials-from-Global-Markets.aspx.

EUROPEAN CENTRAL BANK. 2009. *EU Banking Structures 2008.* Frankfurt: European Central Bank, .

EUROPEAN COMMISSION. 2008. *The raw materials inititive — meeting our critical needs for growth and in jobs in Europe.* Brussels: European Union.

EUROPEAN COMMISSION. 2010. *EUROPE 2020 — A strategy for smart, sustainable and inclusive growth.* COM(2010) 2020. Brussels: European Union.

EUROPEAN COMMISSION. 2011a. *Raw materials — European industry needs access to critical raw materials* [online]. [Accessed July 7th, 2011]. Available from: http://ec.europa.eu/commission_2010-2014/tajani/hot-topics/raw-materials/index_en.htm.

EUROPEAN COMMISSION. 2011b. *Raw materials — Facts and figures* [online]. [Accessed August 13th, 2011]. Available from: http://ec.europa.eu/enterprise/policies/raw-materials/facts-figures/index_en.htm.

EUROPEAN COMMISSION. 2011c. *Raw materials — Public consultation on a possible Innovation Partnership on raw materials* [online]. [Accessed August 14th, 2011]. Available from: http://ec.europa.eu/enterprise/policies/raw-materials/public-consultation-ip/index_en.htm#h2-6.

EUROPEAN COMMISSION. 2011d. *Raw materials — Public consultation on the Raw Materials Initiative* [online]. [Accessed August 13th, 2011]. Available from: http://ec.europa.eu/enterprise/policies/raw-materials/public-consultation/index_en.htm.

EUROPEAN COMMISSION. 2011e. *Tackling the challenges in commodity markets and on raw materials.* Brussels: European Union.

GREAT BRITAIN. 2011f. *Treaty provisions.* European Union.

EUROSTAT. 2011. *Harmonised unemployment rate by gender — total* [online]. [Accessed August 12th, 2011]. Available from: http://epp.eurostat.ec.europa.eu/tgm/table.do?tab=table&language=en&pcode=teilm020&tableSelection=1&plugin=1.

FARREL, D., S. LUND, E. GERLEMAN and P. SEEBURGER. 2007. *The New Power Brokers: How Oil, Asia, Hedge Funds, and Private Equity Are Shaping Global Capital Markets.* McKinsey Global Institute.

FRAZIER, J., K. P. COYNE and J. W. WITTER. 2002. What makes our stock prices go up and down. *McKinsey Quarterly, 2*.

GOLDMAN SACHS. 2008. *Interview with Jim O'Neill* [online]. [Accessed July 10th, 2011]. Available from: http://www2.goldmansachs.com/ideas/brics/index.html

GRIFFITH-JONES, S. and J. A. OCAMPO. 2010. Sovereign Wealth Funds, A developing country perspective. *Foundation for European Progressive Studies*.

GUGLER, P. 2010. World Investment Report 2008: Transnational Corporations and the Infrastructure Challenge, United Nations, New York and Geneva (2008). *International Business Review, 19*(2), p206 — 208.

GUPTA, R., V. TULI and S. VERMA. 2005. Securing - India's energy needs. *McKinsey Quartlery,* (Special edition: Fulfilling India's promise).

HAISENKO, P. 2010. *"Cumulative Current Account Balance" — Wie gefährlich ist Irlands Staatsverschuldung?* [online]. [Accessed July 12th, 2011]. Available from: http://www.gt-worldwide.com/irland_staatsverschuldung_euro.html.

HAJKOWICZ, S. and J. MOODY. 2010. *Our Future World — An analysis of global trends, shocks and scenarios.* Clayton South: Commonwealth Scientific and Industrial Research Organisation

HUANG, S.-L., C.-T. YEH and L.-F. CHANG. 2010. The transition to an urbanizing world and the demand for natural resources. *Current Opinion in Environmental Sustainability,* **2**(3), p136 —143.

INTERNATIONAL MONETARY FUND. 2011a. *Currency Composition of Official Foreign Exchange Reserves (COFER)* [online]. [Accessed August 17th, 2011]. Available from: http://www.imf.org/external/np/sta/cofer/eng/cofer.pdf.

INTERNATIONAL MONETARY FUND. 2011b. *Data Template on International Reserves and Foreign Currency Liquidity* [online]. [Accessed July 14th, 2011]. Available from: http://www.imf.org/external/np/sta/ir/IRProcessWeb/colist.aspx.

JEN, S. 2007. Sovereign Wealth Funds: What they are and what's happening *World Economics,* **8**(4).

JOHNSON, G., K. SCHOLES and R. WHITTINGTON. eds. 2008. *Exploring Corporate strategy* Harlow: Prentice Hall.

KABERUKA, D. 2010. Capturing Africa's buiness opportunity. *McKinsey Quarterly,* (June).

KERN, S. 2007a. Sovereign wealth funds state investments on the rise. *Deutsche Bank Research* (Current Issues).

KERN, S. 2007b. Staatsfonds — Staatliche Auslandsinvestionen im Aufwind. *Deutsche Bank Research* (405).

KERN, S. 2008. Finanzdienstleister — Staatsfonds auf Einkaustour. *Deutsche Bank Research* (23).

KIKUCHI, M. and H. NAGAYOSHI. 2008. LDP's SWF concept. *Merrill Lynch — Japan Strategy Memo.*

KIRKLAND. 2009. A new world disorder — Political-risk consultant Ian Bremer discusses how the downturn is reshaping globalization. *McKinsey Quarterly,* **March**.

KÖHLER, H. 2011. *"Ich dachte, ich könnte helfen"* [online]. [Accessed June 30th, 2011]. Available from: http://www.zeit.de/2011/24/Interview-Koehler/seite-2.

KORNAI, J. 2000. What the Change of System From Socialism to Capitalism Does and Does Not Mean. *Journal of Economic Perspectives,* **14**(1-Winter), p27—42.

KOTTER, J. and U. LEL. 2011. Friends or foes? Target selection decisions of sovereign wealth funds and their consequences. *Journal of Financial Economics,* **101**(2), p360 — 381.

LAEVEN, L. 2010. The Investment Allocation of Sovereign Wealth Funds. *In: Committee on Global Though - "Sovereign Wealth Funds and other long-term investors" Columbia University, New York, NY.* International Monetary Fund

LEKE, A., S. LUND, C. ROXBURGH and A. V. WAMELEN. 2010. What's driving Africa's growth. *McKinsey Quarterly,* (June).

LÓPEZ, R. 2010. *World Economic Crises: Commodity Prices and Environmental Scarcity as Missing Links.* thesis, University of Maryland at College Park.

LUEDI, T. 2008. China's track record in M&A. *McKinsey Quarterly,* (Number 3).

MEYER, T. 2011. *Mission* [online]. [Accessed July 12th, 2011]. Available from: http://www.dbresearch.de/servlet/reweb2.ReWEB?rwnode=DBR_INTERNET_EN-PROD$RSNN0000000000136565&rwsite=DBR_INTERNET_EN-PROD.

NEUBERGER, D., M. ECKHARDT, S. RÄTHKE and E. ANDREANI. 2002. *Intermediäre auf den Markt für Finanzdienstleistung* [online]. [Accessed July 5th, 2011]. Available from: http://www.wiwi.uni-rostock.de/fileadmin/Institute/VWL/VWL-Institut/Poster/PDF/Finanzintermediation_und_Finanzsystem_01.pdf.

NORD STREAM. 2011a. *Company* [online]. [Accessed August 13th, 2011]. Available from: http://www.nord-stream.com/en/our-company.html.

NORD STREAM. 2011b. *Home — Nord Stream* [online]. [Accessed August 13th, 2011]. Available from: http://www.nord-stream.com/en.html?no_cache=1.

NORGES BANK INVESTMENT MANAGEMENT. 2011. *Investments Asset Mix* [online]. [Accessed August 15th, 2011]. Available from: http://www.nbim.no/en/Investments/asset-mix/.

O'NEILL, J., D. WILSON, R. PURUSHOTHAMAN and A. STUPNYTSKA. 2005. How Solid are the BRICs? *Goldman Sachs — Global Economics,* (Paper No. 134).

OBERTHÜR, T. 2011. *Mineral Resources* [online]. [Accessed July 4th, 2011]. Available from: http://www.bgr.bund.de/EN/Themen/Min_rohstoffe/min_rohstoffe_node_en.html.

PETRO STRATEGIES INCORPORATION. 2011. *Leading Oil and Gas Companies Around the World* [online]. [Accessed July 14th, 2011]. Available from:

http://www.petrostrategies.org/Links/Worlds_Largest_Oil_and_Gas_Companie
s_Sites.htm.

REES, J. 1990. *Natural Resources: Allocation, Economics and Policy.* Routledge.

RESERVE BANK OF INDIA. 2011. *2. Foreign Exchange Reserves* [online].
[Accessed July 14th, 2011]. Available from:
http://rbidocs.rbi.org.in/rdocs/Wss/PDFs/25241.pdf.

ROBERT BOSCH. 2011. *Sustainability — Megatrends* [online]. [Accessed July 1st,
2011]. Available from:
http://www.bosch.com/en/com/sustainability/issues/corporate_leadership/meg
atrends_2/megatrends.html.

SAUNDERS, M., P. LEWIS and A. THORNHILL. 2009. *Research methods for
business students.* Pearson Education Limited.

SCHOAR, A. and M. KOERNER. 2010. The Investment Strategies of Sovereign
Wealth Funds. *In: Committee on Global Though — "Sovereign Wealth Funds
and other long-term investors", Columbia University, New York, NY.* Sloan
School of Management Massachusetts Institute of Technology

SHEMIRANI, M. 2011. *Sovereign Wealth Funds and International Political Economy.*
Surrey: Ashgate Publishing Limited.

SHEN, L., S. CHENG, A. J. GUNSON and H. WAN. 2005. Urbanization,
sustainability and the utilization of energy and mineral resources in China.
Cities, **22**(4), p287 — 302.

SKILLING, D. 2009. New challenges for Asia's governments. *McKinsey Quarterly,*
(Number 3).

SMITH, A. ed. 1976. *The Wealth of Nations.* Chicago: The University of Chicago
Press.

SPIEGEL. 2011. *Europas Jugend ohne Zukunft* [online]. [Accessed August 11th,
2011]. Available from:
http://www.spiegel.de/wirtschaft/soziales/0,1518,779610,00.html.

STIFTUNG HAUS DER GESCHICHTE DER BUNDESREPUBLIK DEUTSCHLAND.
2011. *Biografie: Horst Köhler* [online]. [Accessed July 14th, 2011]. Available
from: http://www.hdg.de/lemo/html/biografien/KoehlerHorst/index.html.

SUWAIDI, H., CARUANA J. 2008. Sovereign Wealth Funds, Generally Accepted
Principles and Practices, "Santiago Principles". *International Working Group
on Sovereign Wealth Funds*

SWF INSTITUTE. 2008. *Statistics & Research* [online]. [Accessed September 24th,
2008]. Available from:
http://www.swfinstitute.org/research/strategytransparency.php.

SWF INSTITUTE. 2011. *Sovereign Wealth Fund Rankings* [online]. [Accessed April 25th, 2011]. Available from: http://www.swfinstitute.org/fund-rankings/.

TAGESSCHAU. 2011. *Zwischen Hungersnot und Wirtschaftsinteressen* [online]. [Accessed July 12th, 2011]. Available from: http://www.tagesschau.de/ausland/merkelkenia100.html.

TAJANI, A. 2011. *Raw materials — European industry needs access to critical raw materials* [online]. [Accessed July 7th, 2011]. Available from: http://ec.europa.eu/commission_2010-2014/tajani/hot-topics/raw-materials/index_en.htm.

TRUMAN, E. M. 2010. *Sovereign Wealth Funds: Threat or Salvation?* . 1st ed. Washington, DC: Peter G. Peterson Institute for International Economics.

TWICKEL, C. 2011. Krawalle in England — "Diese Regierung hat die Zivilgesellschaft zerstört". *Spiegel Online*

UNITED NATIONS. 2010a. *World Investment Report 2010 — Investing in a low-carbon economy.* Geneva: United Nations.

UNITED NATIONS. 2010b. *World Urbanization Prospects* New York: United Nations — Department of Economics and Social Affairs.

UNITED STATES CONGRESS HOUSE OF REPRESENTATIVES. 2008. *Sovereign Wealth Funds: New challenges from a changing landscape.* Washington: U.S. Government Printing Offices.

UNITED STATES GENERAL ACCOUNTING OFFICE. 1996. *Foreign Investments — Foreign Laws and Policies Addressing National Security Concerns* United States General Accounting Offices.

VISSER, P. S., J. A. KROSNICK, J. MARQUETTE and M. CURTIN. 1996. Mail surveys for election forecasting? An Evaluation of the Columbus Dispatch Poll. *Public Option Quarterly,* **60**, p181 — 227.

WILSON, D. and R. PURUSHOTHAMAN. 2003. Dreaming with BRICs: The Path to 2050. *Goldman Sachs — Global Economics,* **Paper No. 99**.

WOLNICKI, M. 2010. The day after neoliberal triumphalism. *International Journal of Social Economics,* **37**(7), p476 — 487.

WORLD BANK. 2011. *Commodity Markets* [online]. [Accessed June 30th, 2011]. Available from: http://econ.worldbank.org/WBSITE/EXTERNAL/EXTDEC/EXTDECPROSPECTS/0,,contentMDK:21574907~menuPK:7859231~pagePK:64165401~piPK:64165026~theSitePK:476883,00.html.

WORLD TRADE ORGANIZATION. 2011. *Dispute Settlement — Panel reports out on China's export measures on various raw materials* [online]. [Accessed June 30th, 2011]. Available from:
http://www.wto.org/english/tratop_e/dispu_e/cases_e/ds394_e.htm#bkmk394r.

ZHAO, X. and S. ZHANG. 2006. *Report on China's Foreign Exchange Reserves.* Beijing: School of Finance Renmin University of China.

8 Appendices

Appendix 1: SWF survey

**Leeds University
Business School**

UNIVERSITY OF LEEDS

Survey – SWF Investments

This survey is being carried out to evaluate your thinking about the development of natural resources especially in terms of minerals and metals. Furthermore your opinion about the relevance and your activities in these fields is being questioned.

ALL THE INFORMATION YOU PROVIDE WILL BE TREATED HIGHLY CONFIDENTIAL. THE RESULTS OF THE SURVEY WILL BE USED ANONYMOUSLY ONLY.

The questionnaire should take you about five minutes to complete. Please answer the questions by ticking the appropriate box. Please tick only one box. If you like you can make individual comments in the space provided.

WHEN YOU COMPLETED THE QUESTIONANAIRE, PLEASE RETURN IT TO US PER EMAIL NO LATER THAN 29 JULY.

If you have any queries or would like to have further information about this project, please call me on +49 174 9392937 or email me to **bn09m4t@leeds.ac.uk**

Thank you for your help

Marcel Tiemann
The University of Leeds
Centre for International Business (CIBUL)
Maurice Keyworth Building
Leeds, LS2 9JT
United Kingdom

http://lubswww.leeds.ac.uk/cibul/

Leeds University
Business School

UNIVERSITY OF LEEDS

1. How do you evaluate the development concerning the amount of your fund´s investments within the next 3 years?

Please tick the appropriate box:	Increase	Decrease	Remaining the sum	Not sure
	◯	◯	◯	◯

Comments:

2. What kind of entry strategies does your fund prefer? (If the company is not listed)

Please tick the appropriate box:	IPO	Strategic Sales	Trade Sales
	◯	◯	◯

Comments:

3. Acquisition method used for the investments

Please tick the appropriate box:	Tender offer	Open market purchase	Privately negotiated	Other
	◯	◯	◯	◯

Comments:

4. Future economic growth is threatened by a scarcity of natural resources especially in terms of minerals and metals.

Please tick the appropriate box:	Strongly agree	Agree	Disagree	Strongly disagree
	◯	◯	◯	◯

Comments:

2/7

Leeds University
Business School

UNIVERSITY OF LEEDS

5. The price of natural resources especially in terms of minerals and metals. in the next years will increase strongly

	Strongly agree	Agree	Disagree	Strongly disagree
Please tick the appropriate box:	○	○	○	○

Comments:

6. Do you evaluate an investment in natural resources especially minerals and metals as a very good investment?

	Strongly agree	Agree	Disagree	Strongly disagree
Please tick the appropriate box:	○	○	○	○

Comments:

7. How many investments has your fund made within the last 3 years in natural resources?

	Number of investments in natural resources	Investment volume in natural resources
Please type in:		
	Number of investments in minerals and metals	Investment volume in minerals and metals
Please type in:		

Comments:

8. How many investments has your fund made within the last 5 years?

Please type in:

Number of investments in natural resources	Investment volume in natural resources

Please type in:

Number of investments in minerals and metals	Investment volume in minerals and metals

Comments:

**Leeds University
Business School**

UNIVERSITY OF LEEDS

9. **Could you split the number of investments and the investment volume into regions?**

Natural resources				
Please type in:	In the last 3 years		In the last 5 five years	
Region	Number	Amount	Number	Amount
Asia (excluding India and China)				
China				
India				
Africa				
Australia				
Latin America				
North America				
Europe				

Comments:

5/7

Metals and minerals				
Please type in:	In the last 3 years		In the last 5 five years	
Region	Number	Amount	Number	Amount
Asia (excluding India and China)				
China				
India				
Africa				
Australia				
Latin America				
North America				
Europe				

Comments:

6/7

Leeds University
Business School

I hope you find completing the questionnaire enjoyable. Thank you very much for taking the time to help us. If you would like to receive the final work of this survey please tick the following box.

I would like to receive the final work: ☐ Yes

General comments:

Thank you for your help.

Marcel Tiemann
Centre for International Business (CIBUL)

Appendix 2: Research experts' survey

**Leeds University
Business School**

This survey is being carried out to evaluate your thinking about the importance and relevance of natural resources, especially in terms of minerals and metals for European Union´s economic growth. Furthermore your opinion about the necessity of governmental interaction to extend the European Union 2020 Strategy for smart, sustainable and inclusive growth is being questioned.

ALL THE INFORMATION YOU PROVIDE WILL BE TREATED HIGHLY CONFIDENTIAL. THE RESULTS OF THE SURVEY WILL BE USED ANONYMOUSLY ONLY.

The questionnaire should take you about five minutes to complete. Please answer the questions by ticking the appropriate box. Please tick only one box. If you like you can make individual comments in the space provided. Your answers are essential to verify an alternative approach to the European Union Strategy 2020.

WHEN YOU HAVE COMPLETED THE QUESTIONANAIRE, PLEASE RETURN IT TO US PER EMAIL NO LATER THAN 29 JULY.

If you have any queries or would like to have further information about this project, please call me on +49 174 9392937 or email me to **bn09m4t@leeds.ac.uk**

Thank you for your help

Marcel Tiemann
The University of Leeds
Centre for International Business (CIBUL)
Maurice Keyworth Building
Leeds, LS2 9JT
United Kingdom

1/4

**Leeds University
Business School**

1. What is your opinion to the following statement? 'The EU´s future economic growth is threatened by a scarcity of natural resources especially in terms of minerals and metals.

	Strongly agree	Agree	Disagree	Strongly disagree
Please tick the appropriate box:	◯	◯	◯	◯

Comments:

2. How do you think about the following statement? '**Governments should take an important and active role to secure access to critical resources especially minerals and metals'**

	Strongly agree	Agree	Disagree	Strongly disagree
Please tick the appropriate box:	◯	◯	◯	◯

Comments:

3. '**Developing and transition economies take advantage through governmental investments in minerals and metals'** How strong do you agree to this statement?

	Strongly agree	Agree	Disagree	Strongly disagree
Please tick the appropriate box:	◯	◯	◯	◯

Comments:

2/4

**Leeds University
Business School**

UNIVERSITY OF LEEDS

4. **'Sovereign Wealth Funds are state-owned investment vehicles which invest strongly in minerals and metals'** Tick the box that matches your view most closely.

	Strongly agree	Agree	Disagree	Strongly disagree
Please tick the appropriate box:	◯	◯	◯	◯

Comments:

5. How do you think about the following statement? **'European Union (EU) is a conglomerate of national states who speak and act with one voice'**

	Strongly agree	Agree	Disagree	Strongly disagree
Please tick the appropriate box:	◯	◯	◯	◯

Comments:

6. How is your acceptance of the following statement? **'European Union (EU) is able to operate together in financial and economical affairs'**

	Strongly agree	Agree	Disagree	Strongly disagree
Please tick the appropriate box:	◯	◯	◯	◯

Comments:

3/4

Leeds University
Business School

UNIVERSITY OF LEEDS

7. What is your opinion to the following statement? **'The European Union (EU) should increase their activities to invest directly to procure natural resources'**

Please tick the appropriate box:	Strongly agree	Agree	Disagree	Strongly disagree
	○	○	○	○

Comments:

8. **'A "European Union SWF" could be an adequate instrument to ensure direct access to natural resources'** Tick the box that matches your view most closely

Please tick the appropriate box:	Strongly agree	Agree	Disagree	Strongly disagree
	○	○	○	○

Comments:

I hope you find completing the questionnaire enjoyable. Thank you very much for taking the time to help us. If you would like to receipt the final work of this survey please tick the following box.

I would like to receive the final work: ☐ Yes

General comments:

Thank you for your help.

Marcel Tiemann
Centre for International Business (CIBUL)

4/4

Appendix 3: Results of the survey

respondents	Q1	Q2	Q3	Q4	Q5	Q6	Q7	Q8
1	3.0	3.0	2.0	3.0	0.0	1.0	4.0	4.0
2	3.0	3.0	2.0	3.0	4.0	4.0	3.0	3.0
3	3.0	4.0	3.0	4.0	3.0	3.0	3.0	4.0
4	4.0	3.0	2.0	2.0	3.0	3.0	4.0	4.0
5	3.0	2.0	2.0	2.0	3.0	2.0	3.0	4.0
6	3.0	2.0	2.0	2.0	3.0	2.0	3.0	3.0
7	3.0	3.0	3.0	3.0	3.0	3.0	3.0	3.0
8	2.0	1.0	1.0	2.0	3.0	3.0	2.0	3.0
9	2.0	2.0	2.0	3.0	3.0	2.0	2.0	3.0
10	3.0	2.0	2.0	3.0	3.0	2.0	3.0	3.0
11	2.0	1.0	1.0	1.0	3.0	4.0	1.0	3.0
mean	**2.8**	**2.4**	**2.0**	**2.5**	**3.1**	**2.6**	**2.8**	**3.4**
σ	0.57	0.88	0.60	0.78	0.30	0.88	0.83	0.48
n=33								

Appendix 4: Santiago Principles – GAAP

1) Sound legal framework	13) Clearly defined professional and ethical standards
2) Clearly defined policy purpose	14) No inappropriate influence from third parties
3) Coordination with domestic fiscal and monetary authorities	15) Comply with host country regulations
4) Clear policies regarding funding, withdrawal, spending	16) Public disclosure of governance framework
5) Timely reporting	17) Publicly disclosed financial information
6) Sound governance	18) Sound portfolio management principles
7) Oversight and objectives by a governing body	19) Investment decisions to maximize returns only
8) Adequate authority for governing bodies	20) Do not seek priviledged info or undue influence
9) Independent operational management	21) Respect for shareholder ownership rights
10) Clearly defined accountability framework	22) Framework for risk management
11) Annual report that adheres to national standards	23) Reporting of assets and investment
12) Annual audit	24) Regular review of GAPP implementation

Some clear and enunciated purposes (in explanation and commentary):

1. "Clear **delineation of responsibilities between the SWF and other governmental entities**"
2. "SWF undertakes investments **without any intention or obligation to fulfill directly or indirectly any geopolitical agenda of the government**"
6. "Operational management should be conducted...**in effect free of political influence or interference**"
9. "The operational management should act in the best interest of the SWF"
11. "This is important to ensure that information about investments and performance is clear, fair, accurate"
12. "The audit procedure should be open for review"
13. "Staff should be appropriately qualified and well-trained, and should be subject to minimum professional standards"
15. "It is essential that the **SWF respect host country rules** and comply with all applicable laws and regulations of host countries in which SWF operations are conducted"
17. "...Asset allocation, benchmarks... to contribute to stability in international financial markets and **enhance trust in recipient countries**"
20. "**SWFs should not seek advantages** such as those arising from **privileged** access to **market sensitive information**"
21. SWFs should **disclose *ex ante* whether and how they exercise their voting rights**.

Figure 27: The Santiago Principles (Bolton and Samama 2010)

Appendix 5: The theory of financial intermediation

The theory of financial intermediation states that markets are complex systems which are characterized by imperfectness such as lack of information or transaction costs. In this system banks have an intermediate function which could lead to a better economic situation. They provide a transformation service to reduce costs for lack of information and asymmetric information (Neuberger *et al.* 2002). This role is illustrated in figure 28.

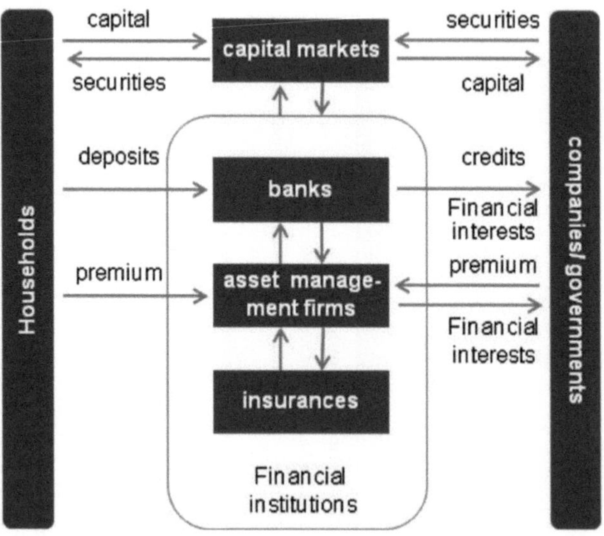

Figure 28: The role of financial institutions in the markets (Neuberger *et al.* 2002, p. 1)

Appendix 6: The sustainable strategy of the EU

The sustainable strategy of the EU for smart, sustainable and inclusive growth is based on the following three reinforcing priorities:

- Smart growth: developing an economy based on knowledge and innovation
- Sustainable growth: promoting a more resource-efficient, greener and more competitive economy
- Inclusive growth: fostering a high-employment economy delivering social and territorial cohesion (European Commission 2010, pp. 2-7)